D0450713

Chocolate Chili Pepper Love

Becky Freeman

HARVEST HOUSE PUBLISHERS
Eugene, Oregon 97402

Cover by Koechel Peterson & Associates, Minneapolis, Minnesota

CHOCOLATE CHILI PEPPER LOVE

Copyright © 2000 by Becky Freeman
Published by Harvest House Publishers
Eugene, Oregon 97402

Library of Congress Cataloging-in-Publication Data
Freeman, Becky, 1959–
    Chocolate chili pepper love / Becky Freeman
      p. cm.
    ISBN 0-7369-0237-6
    1. Marriage. 2. Marriage—Religious aspects—Christianity. 3. Marriage—Humor. 4. Married people—Psychology. I. Title.
HQ734.F7477   2000
306.81—dc21   99-047424
                                                                                          CIP

Printed in the United States of America

        00   01   02   03   04   05   06   / BP /   10   9   8   7   6   5   4   3

For my best friend and lover,
my Chocolate Chili Pepper husband,
Scott

Acknowledgments

Heartfelt gratitude to:

The *Home Life* staff, for allowing me the privilege of writing the "Marriage 911" column—and for offering prayers and patience through "real life" bumps.

My agent, Greg Johnson, who believes in my work and good-naturedly puts up with my nonstop flow of ideas. He is the Focusing Friend God knew this right-brained writer needed.

Chip MacGregor, who championed this project at Harvest House and who provokes me to outlandish laughter in unsuspecting moments.

Betty Fletcher, topnotch editor and encourager.

Bill and Anabel Gillham—whose words and life message came at a crucial point in our marriage. This book might have been Chocolate Chili Pepper Disaster without their practical and spiritual insights on lasting relationships.

Coyle Stephenson and Brenda Waggoner: friends, counselors, and spiritual advisers to Scott and me in this journey of life, parenting, and marriage.

My husband, Scott, who with amazing grace allows me to open the pages of our lives: the good, the bad, and the crazy.

Contents

Part VII
Forever and Always
Becoming soulmates

On a personal note...

My daughter, coltish and lovely at 15, sat next to me on the wave-washed beach as I scribbled notes and quotes.

"Rachel, I'm writing another book about marriage," I said, peering at her over my sunglasses. "Do you think I'm being a hypocrite?" Through the years, our children have too often been the reluctant white-knuckled riders on the roller coaster of our marriage.

"Not as long as you tell the truth," she answered thoughtfully.

"And what is the truth?"

"That you two are crazy."

"Hey!" I yelped in mock protest, "We're not crazy, we're *unique*."

"Okay, well...then say you and Daddy have had lots of really hard times, but that you've always found a way to love each other again."

And so, I write this book, not as a professional counselor nor as someone with an exemplary marriage. I write as a wife so acquainted with the pain of a marriage-in-process that I'm filled with compassion for anyone struggling up the daunting mountain of committed love. If I offer words of healing, they are born from experience, from stumbling and lurching about in search of wisdom and relief.

Writer Anne Lamott says the most profound prayers are "Help, help, help" and "Thank you, thank you, thank you."[1] For those who may be praying "Help, help, help," I want to assure you there is a compassionate Guide who is listening, a Shepherd on the lookout for His stubborn, lost sheep who are bleating for a better relationship.

So follow along with me as we take a wild journey through the valleys and hills of a typical high maintenance, spicy-sweet marriage. Love, laughter, hope—and help, help, help—are on the way, way, way!

◆ ◆ ◆

As a shepherd looks after his scattered flock when he is with them, so will I look after my sheep. I will rescue them from all the places where they were scattered on a day of clouds and darkness.

EZEKIEL 34:12

Nobody, but nobody, can make it out here alone.

—**Maya Angelou**

Part I

◆ ◆ ◆

Women Are from Neiman's, Men from Home Depot

Compatibility for couples with nothing in common

1

What Flavor Is Your Marriage?

Did you know that marriages usually come in one of three flavors?

It's true.

Couples come in three varieties: vanilla, strawberry, and chocolate chili pepper. All of them can be delicious. None of the three is superior to the other. It's all a matter of taste. However, all three flavors can spoil if they're not properly tended.

I discovered these flavorful facts while reading a fascinating book called *Why Marriages Succeed or Fail* by Dr. John Gottman. Of course, Dr. Gottman refers to the three marital types as being either avoidant, validating, or volatile. But somehow vanilla, strawberry, and chocolate chili pepper sounded more fun to me.

How do you determine what flavor you are? Well, if you minimize conflict—using the dodging and hedging technique, making light of most differences rather than resolving them, you're probably the proud owners of a consistent, tasty, good ol' Vanilla Bean Marriage. (You're what Dr. Gottman terms an avoidant couple.) These stable couples tend to accentuate the positive in their relationship and agree to disagree about the rest. They value their own space and lead calm, pleasant lives alongside each other but not always *with* each other. In a word, they are comfy.

If, however, you and your spouse are virtuosos at communication, openly display affection, and share time and activities and interests with each other, you're a marriage counselor's dream. And you probably enjoy a fruity, yummy, Strawberry Marriage. (Or in Dr. Gottman's words, you are a validating couple.) Strawberry types try to persuade each other to the rightness of their position, usually ending up in a compromise. They often complete each other's sentences, value togetherness, enjoy a "we-ness" in their marriage. (An aside. True confession: At a ladies retreat I read this explanation aloud and when murmurs and laugher rolled through the audience I finally asked, "What's so funny?" To my embarrassment, the women had misunderstood the word "we-ness"—thinking I'd said, instead, the name of… um… a vital male organ.)

And then, oh my, there's the rest of us. We fight on a grand scale—but often have an even grander time making up. An "uninvolved or withdrawn partner" does not exist ANYWHERE in this highly flavorful flavor. Stubborn R Us. In the heat (and I do mean heat) of an argument, we have little interest in hearing the other's point of view. Right off, a marriage counselor will observe that these couples tend to say "Yes, you do!" and "No, I don't!" more often than "Mm-hmm" and "I see." They fight and love and laugh out loud. Picture author Leo Buscaglia's large Italian family—or the family from the movie *Moonstruck*. Hugs, shouting, intensity, tears, and hilarity can all pour forth from one family spaghetti dinner.

If this sounds like your marriage, welcome to the spicy, doubled-dipped flavor: chocolate chili pepper. We're noisy. Dr. Gottman refers to us as the volatile couples. We're interesting, to be sure, but you have to keep a watchful eye on us peppery types. In fact, I'm convinced these wild, high maintenance relationships simply take more life-long tending than the other types of marriages.

The other night I went out to a restaurant with my sister Rachel, whose quick wit sometimes catches me off guard. The waiter asked, "Are there just two of you in the party?" Before I could answer in the affirmative, my sister interjected, half apologizing, "Yes, but we're a real handful." So it is with especially stubborn or melancholy or creative couples. There may be only two of you in the party, but let's face facts: You're probably going to be quite a handful.

Every mother of a strong-willed child knows there are some kids who are simply more work to raise than others. The toddler-worn mother is the one helplessly trying to explain why her offspring is spreading jelly across the piano keys to another mother whose calm, compliant prodigy is sitting quietly on the floor leafing through a cloth booklet of the Greek alphabet. Dr. James Dobson relieved the collective guilt of half this country's mothers when he wrote the book, *The Strong-Willed Child*, assuring parents that children enter this world with very different personalities. Some babies burst out of the womb and into the labor room ordering the doctor to, "Hurry up with those scissors and cut that cord! I have places to go, nurses to aggravate!" Other children come gently into this world, slipping effortlessly through the birth canal with angelic smiles on their faces asking, "And what else can I do to help you, Mother?"

Until Dr. Dobson writes a lawfully (or awfully) wedded sequel, *The Strong-Willed Marriage*, I offer to my fellow chocolate chili pepper strugglers the following hopeful conclusion to Dr. Gottman's fascinating research.

When Gottman set out to discover what determines the success or failure of a marriage, he thought he might find the one type—assumably the validating (strawberry) type—that would win the Most Likely To Succeed Award. Surprisingly, he found healthy, happy couples in all three categories. The difference between success and failure—statistically speaking—boiled down to The Five-to-One Ratio Indicator.

If a couple reported an average of five good times vs. one rotten time in their marriage, their chances of staying together in happy matrimony soared. This was a comforting study to me in that I realized Scott and I don't have to keep striving to be The Ideal Couple. We can be our own peculiar "us"—but we must pay attention to putting good stuff in our marriage bank account: at least five happy events to one yucky one. Neglect a relationship and any marriage will stall. There's no *neutral* in marriage; it's either in *drive* or *reverse*. If two people purpose to nurture their marriage with happy thoughts, events, and experiences—that marriage, whatever variety, will go forward.

Stable couples of all flavors put more weight on the positive side of their marriage equation. Research found, for example:

- *They showed an active interest in one another.*
- *They showed affection—even if it was low-key.*
- *They did small thoughtful acts for one another; they showed appreciation, concern, and empathy.*
- *They were accepting of each other's good points and weaknesses.*

- *They joked around and when they felt a burst of joy or excitement they let their partner know it.*

I don't know about you, but this encourages me to work on putting at least a month's worth of "happy stuff" into our "volatile marriage" bank. Maybe we can go a little heavier on the chocolate and lighter on the chili pepper.

It's my hope and prayer that these essays from one imperfect, but determined, high-maintenance partner will help you accept the marriage you have and quit envying other couples who have easier or more proper "flavors." Along the way, I'll offer practical ways to fill your marriage with at least fivefold more good times than bad.

So here's to vanilla, strawberry, and chocolate chili peppers alike! May your own unique cup overflow with lifelong love.

◆ ◆ ◆

He who refreshes others will himself be refreshed.

PROVERBS 11:25

*They do not love
that do not show their love.*

—William Shakespeare

2

My Husband, the Hero

Hey, ladies, do you remember the first hero that made your little heart pitter-patter? I was six when I found myself lovestruck over a cartoon rendition of Hercules. He was, I thought, the most handsome and well-drawn figure of a man I'd ever seen. I would daydream of being whisked away from my kindergarten-small-potato-life in the arms of my cartoon hunk.

Then one day I realized my cartoon hero from Mount Olympus was much too one-dimensional. What I needed was a real man. A swinger. A man who knew how to hold meaningful conversations, even if they were with a chimpanzee. I practiced swinging from the cross bar on my jungle gym until I was sure that if Tarzan ever happened by and noted how graceful I was, he'd drop Jane faster than a slick banana. Then came Superman. Followed by Prince Charming and on it went until the summer of 1974.

Enter Scott.

He and I were teenagers, old friends from church, who decided to serve the Lord on a summer mission trip to El Salvador. But before we could go to Central America, we'd have to survive Boot Camp in the swamplands of Florida. Upon our arrival at what appeared to be a refugee tent city, I turned to Scott hopefully and asked, "Where do you suppose is my condo?"

He grinned and squashed a mosquito the size of a small Chihuahua hungrily sucking blood from my arm.

"This is great!" he beamed, and I realized with awe that he actually meant it. Soft-spoken, mild-mannered Scott Freeman transformed before my very eyes into MacGyver and Rambo combined. And I, Miss Teen Femininity, would soon find myself living in denim overalls and army boots. Little did I realize how long it would be before I enjoyed a hot bath or air conditioning again. At that moment it became clear: Only one of us was a genuinely happy camper.

After settling into a tent with several other girls, I waited eagerly for dinner. I was famished. But as soon as the server handed me a tin bowl of chili, I tripped over my new boots and deposited most of my one-course dinner on a fellow teammate's back. I did the best I could to scrape the beans off his shoulder with my spoon.

"I guess that's why they call it a mess hall," I offered. Looking around to see who had observed my graceful dive, I saw Scott grinning at me from his seat in the corner of the makeshift dining hall. I blushed clear down to my steel-tipped toes.

I'd lived to the ripe old age of 15, and accidents like spilling chili down a stranger's neck were already fairly common to me. I usually took them in stride, but this time was different. A whole new set of thoughts tripped into my dithered head.

Scott looks so tall. Has he always been so handsome?

He stood up slowly, stretched to his full six feet, glided toward me with the litheness of a cat—and walked face first into a tent pole.

Oh, my goodness! my heart beat wildly. *He's perfect!*

The next morning, Scott led our team in a workout that left me feeling like a wad of chewed gum. Too late, I remembered he had taken gymnastics for years, which may have accounted for his Adonis build. Even in the dim light of dawn, I could see his tan, his perfect white teeth, the straight golden brown hair falling over doe brown eyes, the square chin...

By the end of the week, with Scott's heroic leadership, our ragtag unit completed the obstacle course and emerged as a united team. After days filled with physical challenges and learning how to tie steel and lay brick, we teens would gather under the big top tent for precious times of worship and refreshment. There was one night in particular I'll never forget.

After an especially moving devotion, I was kneeling in prayer at the front. I happened to glance behind me and saw Scott kneeling there, too. I looked into his face, and he into mine, and it seemed as if the dirt floor became holy ground. Like some ethereal dream, everything around us stopped and quieted and blurred, except for what was clearly happening between us. A delightful thought shot through my mind. *This young man will be your husband someday.*

Then Scott reached for my hand and held it for a few seconds, our gaze unwavering.

"I love you, Becky," he whispered. "Seems like I always have."

"I love you, too." My lips formed the words before my mind could talk my heart out of it. Could it be I was falling in love with a friend? An old buddy? We were fifteen and sixteen! Impossible!

It scares me to say this, now that I have teenagers of my own, but sometimes the impossible happens. At the end of that summer, Scott spent his last $12.00 on a tiny gold band and gave it to me as a sign of friendship. Two years later, he slipped the same ring on my finger again—as a wedding ring.

Now, twenty-one years later, I have to confess: he's my hero—my Prince Charming/Rambo/MacGyver/Hercules/Tarzan husband, Scott. And you should see how gracefully I can still hang from my knees on a jungle gym—as long as my hero husband stands ready to catch me.

Truth is, there's a hero inside every husband. And it's our privilege and challenge to help bring that hero to light.

◆ ◆ ◆

Many times you have miraculously rescued me...You have been loving and kind to me

PSALM 18:50 TLB

I am Tarzan of the Apes. I am yours. You are mine. We will live here together always in my house.

—Edgar Rice Burroughs

3

A Little Less Talk–
A Lot More Action

I nudged my husband during a particularly. poignant scene as I sat in the darkened theater absorbed in the movie, *Enchanted April*. It was a beautifully filmed story about a cluster of nineteenth-century English women vacationing on the coast of Italy. Their conversations were quiet, even furtive, filled with rich hidden meanings. The action was slow, subtle, and lovely. The plot was more concerned with internal blossoming than outward action.

"Isn't this a wonderful movie?" I whispered to my Beloved. The sole reply from Scott was a deep, low snore.

I was disappointed, but not surprised. Whenever I go out for an evening, or speak at a conference for the weekend, Scott rents movies I can't fathom. He likes movies with Stallone and Schwarzenegger types, actors awash in testosterone. Films where copious running, catapulting, and random explosions are the norm. Scenes where seldom is heard a meaningful word, but the firearms boom loudly all day.

When Scott's out of town, on the other hand, I put on a pot of Earl Grey, pop a Jane Austin flick into the VCR, and settle in for a visual feast of crumpets and scones, green fields dotted with cottages, and well-behaved ladies and gentlemen.

These differences in viewing preferences should have clued me in years ago to the fact that men like a little less talk and a lot more action. And yet, through the years, I continued to use the same old standby communication technique common to womankind: talk, talk, and more talk. If the first verbal round failed to accomplish my purpose with Scott, I simply upped the volume and intensity. Once more, with *feeling*.

All to no avail.

Sure, I'd read the third chapter of 1 Peter where the disciple tells wives they can win their husbands over "without a word"—but I assumed this was one of those passages that had to be interpreted according to the customs of biblical times. I didn't realize that Peter was offering a gold mine of wisdom to help women not waste valuable energy on ineffectual approaches to men.

Then I read about a study showing how differently God created the brains of men and women. Males predominantly depend on the left hemisphere of the brain—the side responsible for rational, factual thought and logic. The right hemisphere is responsible for communication skills, feelings, and emotions. Women tend to use both sides equally with great ease. Why? Because the corpus callosum, the delicate fibers connecting the left side of the brain to the right side, is 40 percent larger in women. All right brain functions involving verbal ability, comprehension, and language skills simply come more naturally to women. Michele Weiner-Davis, in her book *A Woman's Guide to Changing Her Man,*[1] suggests women should save their breath and get their feet moving instead, if they want to get a man's attention.

In a nutshell (or should I say "braincell"), ACTION is the key to unlocking a guy's hemisphere. Weiner-Davis, with lighthearted humor, compares men to cats. "If you've ever had a cat," she writes, "you know how single-minded they are about going after moving objects. Anything that wiggles becomes the intense focus of a cat's undivided attention."

Here's a way I used this newfound knowledge in a typical husband-wife standoff. I wanted Scott to hang some extra rods in my closet. I began by leaving the rods on the kitchen counter next to a loving note: "Honey, would you please hang these for me?" Next day, the rods were still on the counter buried under a plate of half-eaten waffles.

So with another nod toward the rods, I tried a verbal request, asking my husband to please install the rods that evening. This proved to be another exercise in futility. Then I remembered that men respond better to action. I had to get something "wiggling."

So the next evening, I took the rods, some bricks, and the largest sledge hammer I could find, went to the closet, and started hammering on the bricks and alternately banging the metal rods together.

Within minutes, my husband—with cat-like response—noticed the "wiggling thing" and proceeded to take over the task. Results?

The rods were installed in less time than it took for a self-satisfied thought to jump from the left to the right side of my brain.

And all it took was a little less talk, and a lot more action.

◆ ◆ ◆

Dear children, let us not love with words or tongue but with actions.

1 JOHN 3:18

A man talks best when he's spraying WD-40 on something or hammering something. Men talk better when they fidget.

—Charles Lowery
Homelife, January 2000

I was tickled to receive this e-mail about some new training courses, perfect for left-brainer-type men in search of their right brain.

Training Courses Now Available for Men

Introduction to Common Household Objects I: The Mop

Introduction to Common Household Objects II: The Sponge

Dressing up: Beyond the Funeral and the Wedding

Refrigerator Forensics: Identifying and Removing the Dead

Design Pattern or Splatter Stain on the Linoleum? You CAN Tell the Difference!

If It's Empty, You Can Throw It Away: Accepting Loss I

If the Milk Expired Three Weeks Ago, Keeping It in the Refrigerator Won't Bring It Back: Accepting Loss II

Going to the Supermarket: It's Not Just for Women Anymore!

Bathroom Etiquette I: How to Remove
Beard Clippings from the Sink

Bathroom Etiquette II: Let's Wash Those
Towels!

Bathroom Etiquette III: Five Easy Ways to
Tell when You're About to Run out of
Toilet Paper!

Giving Back to the Community: How to
Donate 15-Year-Old Levis to the Goodwill

No, the Dishes Won't Wash Themselves:
Knowing the Limitations of Your Kitchen-
ware

Yours, Mine, and Ours: Sharing the
Remote

"I Don't Know": Be the First Man to Say It!

The Gas Gauge in Your Car: Sometimes
Empty MEANS Empty

Directions: It's Okay to Ask for Them

Accepting Your Limitations: Just Because
You Have Power Tools Doesn't Mean You
Can Fix It

4

He Tarzan, Me Jane.
We Friends?

Honey," I sighed as I leaned against the couch. "I feel so ugly and old lately."

"Oh, I know how you feel," Scott started in. "My knees ache, my hair's thinning, my teeth hurt…"

"You just don't get it, do you?" I interrupted.

"Get what?" he asked, bewilderment clouding his eyes.

"Look, when I say, 'I feel so ugly,' that's your big cue to say something nice about me. 'I feel ugly' means 'I need a compliment.'"

Scott shook his head. "I get so confused. I thought 'I feel ugly' was my cue to be empathetic."

I rolled my eyes in exasperation. "Okay, let's go over it again. If I say, 'Honey, I just bounced a check' or 'Scott, I just ran into the mailbox'—*that's* when I want empathy. But if I tell you I feel old and ugly…"

"You want a compliment!"

"Yes!"

"Refresh me again: What kind of compliment?"

"'You grow more beautiful every year' is always a safe bet."

"Oh," Scott replied thoughtfully. "You grow more beautiful every year."

"Thank you," I replied.

Mastering the art of communication with the opposite sex is no easy trick. It takes years of practice, but I believe it begins by accepting two basic truths: "men are not women" and "women are not men." As you can see from the above conversation, Scott has his work cut out for him as he struggles to live with his "wife in an understanding way." I'm also trying my best these days to understand men. Recently, I received a list of "49 Facts About Men" from an alert "Marriage 9-1-1" reader. They were credited to comedienne Rita Rudner. I offer a sampling below with my blessings (and a very wide grin):

- Men like to barbecue. Men will cook if danger is involved.

- Men look nerdy in black socks and sandals.

- Men hate to hear, "We need to talk about our relationship." These seven words could strike fear in the heart of even General Schwarzkopf.

- Men are sensitive in strange ways. If a man builds a fire and the last log doesn't burn, he'll take it personally.

- Most women are introspective: "Am I in love? Am I emotionally and creatively fulfilled?" Most men are outrospective: "Did my team win? How's my car?"

- Men who listen to classical music tend not to spit.

- Men are afraid of eyelash curlers. I sleep with one under my pillow, instead of a gun.

- Men have higher body temperature than women—men are like portable heaters that snore.

- Men love watches with multiple functions. My husband has one that's a combination address book, telescope and piano.

- Men would still really like to own a train set.

Before someone protests, "This is stereotyping men!" may I quickly interject that I believe the third step toward peace between the sexes involves enjoying a good-natured laugh at ourselves. How important it is for us to step back from the Marriage Picture and find humor again in our differences.

I don't know about you, but I'm sick of the ugly battles between men and women. "Male chauvinist!" the feminists accuse. "Male basher!" the men shout back. I long for men and women to come together, to view our differences with smiles of appreciation and curiosity—even though the reality is we'll never *completely* understand each other.

One of the things I love about watching old movies is that I get to peek in at a time when men were men, women were women, and relationships weren't micro-analyzed. I recently watched an old Walt Disney version of *Swiss Family Robinson*. I couldn't help but notice an underlying simplicity, a sweetness between John Robinson and his wife.

I loved the scene where John invites his mate, for the first time, to come and see the tree house he built. As they climb up the ladder together, John's face goes from proud man/survivor to vulnerable little boy—as he waits, wondering what his lady will think of his handiwork. With one sharp word, she could cut his heart in two. She teases him gently at first, but finally lets go—as tears fall freely in appreciation of her husband's efforts. I saw in John, as I see in most men, a basic, wonderful, almost instinctual desire to nurture and protect women—to make them happy. It's just that men have a rather clumsy way of showing this at times. (I find it helps to remember most men are just grown-up little boys with mortgages.)

So we have some differences. Guys barbeque. Gals sauté. Men wear nerdy socks. Women wear old robes.

Men build with Lincoln Logs. Women decorate Dream Houses.

He Tarzan. Me Jane.

But since it gets awfully lonely clinging so tightly to our own vines—whadaya say we swing over to the same tree and make friends again?

◆ ◆ ◆

"A man must...be perfectly joined to his wife, and the two shall be one." I know this is hard to understand...

Ephesians 5:31, 32 tlb

I believe in the difference between men and women. In fact, I embrace the difference.

—Elizabeth Taylor

Things Only Women Understand:

Cats' facial expressions

Fat clothes

Taking a car trip without trying to beat your best time

The difference between beige, off-white, and eggshell

Other Women

Great Reasons to Be a Guy:

A two-week vacation requires only one suitcase.

You can open all your own jars.

Wedding plans take care of themselves.

If someone forgets to invite you to something, he or she can still be your friend.

Your underwear is $10.00 a three-pack.

Everything on your face stays its original color.

You can drop by to see a friend without having to bring a little gift.

You're not expected to know the names of more than five colors.

Christmas shopping can be accomplished for 25 relatives on December 24, in 45 minutes.

5

Funny Girl, Patient Guy

Scott once said he'd love to call a Men-Only meeting with husbands of right-brained humor writers. Among the invited would be at least three Bills: Bill Bombeck (of the late Erma fame), Bill Johnson (of the lively Barbara "Geranium-in-Your-Hat" renown), and Bill Higgs (head of the Liz Curtis Higgs "One-Size-Fits-All" Household). The first thing Scott would most likely say, once he had them cornered, is, "Okay, guys—shoot it to me straight: Have you figured out why the world finds our wives so funny?" For, unless I miss my guess, most of my sisters-in-humor are married to men who don't exactly fall over laughing at the sight of, say, the kids' box turtle snuggled inside their best dress shoe.

I tell a story on myself about the time I could not figure out why the old tin shower in our cabin wouldn't drain. Every time I jumped in to take a shower, the water would fill up and eventually overflow onto the bathroom floor. Weary of my complaining, my husband agreed to observe my dilemma. For strangely enough, I was the only one who seemed to have this problem. So I got in the shower, turned the spigots, and halfway through my scrubdown, sure enough, the water was lapping up and over the rim. I heard Scott muttering. Poking his head through the curtain, he peered at my feet incredulously.

"Becky," Scott asked, "how long have you been standing on the drain?"

When I realized I'd been stopping up the shower for weeks with my own feet, I couldn't wait to phone my best friend and share the laugh. This, too, puzzled my husband. He scratched his head and asked sincerely, "Why would you want to admit—to ANYONE—such ignorance on your part?" "Because," I tried in vain to explain between chuckles, "it's SO FUNNY."

Without a doubt, the story I'm most often asked to share with audiences is dubbed The Lawn Mower Story.

One lovely spring afternoon, Scott asked me to tow him on his riding mower about a mile down the road so he could cut a neighbor's grass. After attaching the mower to the Titanic (my pet name for our station wagon), Scott mounted it, and I carefully began to pull him down the bumpy, oil-topped road.

It was a lovely day, and the wildflowers were just coming into bloom. I was delighted to see how many varieties there were. Before I realized it, my foot had settled into a comfortable forty-miles-per-hour position on the accelerator.

When I happened to glance in the rearview mirror, I saw Scott's elbows flapping up and down like an injured bird in takeoff; I saw six inches of daylight between his posterior and the seat of the tractor and his mouth wide open in a silent scream.

Now, I know I shouldn't have laughed, because…well…I probably could have killed him. But I couldn't help it—he looked SO FUNNY. When I slowed to a stop and Scott dismounted the tractor I could tell by the look on his face he probably didn't see as much humor in the incident as I'd seen. As a matter of fact, all Scott could manage to do was hold his head in his hands and mumble, "Beck-y, Beck-y, Beck-y, Beck-y...."

Whatever natural sense of humor my husband may lack, he more than makes up for it by being a royal good sport. Once he realized I could actually increase the family income by telling the world about all the embarrassing, forgetful and inane things I do, he began to smile a lot more. He's still amazed how God uses "peculiar people" (like his wife) to bring the message of God's love, wrapped up in a tortilla of laughter, to others. And though Scott will probably never get as tickled as I do when I flub up, I hope he—along with Erma's, Liz's and Barbara's Bills—gets an award in heaven, for the special patience it takes to live with a woman who makes a living and/or a ministry out of making messes.

◆ ◆ ◆

Some of our women amazed us...

LUKE 24:22

Blessed is he who has learned to laugh at himself, for he shall never cease to be entertained.

—John Powell

6

The Weighty Matters of Marriage

By far the biggest difference between Scott and me is this: Scott is tall and thin—he works out with weights and runs for the sheer pleasure of staying in shape. I'm short and—let's just say I'm currently reading my 1,789th diet book for the sheer pleasure of imagining what I might look like if I ever do get in shape. If reading books about losing weight would somehow do the trick, I'd currently be the size of a coffee stirrer.

A while back, I lunched with three friends—Linda, Lori, and Mimi. Whatever possessed me to accept an invitation to dine with three women whose combined total weight is probably less than that of my salad plate, I'll never know. The conversation turned to weight control, as it always does when women are eating out. Linda began her pep talk.

"Becky, you've got to start running. I feel so great about myself since I've started jogging—it's unbelievable." Mimi nodded in agreement, "Yes, it's given me a real feeling of power." She paused to flex her beautifully tanned biceps and added, "We are woman, hear us roar!"

With so much energy surging in the atmosphere around me, I suddenly had the overpowering urge to take a nap. I am woman, hear me snore.

I noticed Lori was quiet during the cheerleading, and though she's about the size of a trim gnat, I knew we shared a dislike of habitual exercise. So when Linda complained that she hated to take off two weeks from her running schedule for a needed surgery, Lori leaned in my direction and covered her mouth with her napkin. "I don't know about you," she whispered softly, "but I'd rather have the surgery." I couldn't have agreed more. However, I couldn't argue with the results. Linda and Mimi are stunning. And shouldn't Scott have a thin, athletic, roaring wife too? So, I decided to start running.

On Day One, my athletic son, Zeke, watching my jogging warm-up, tried to gain control of himself. I ignored his guffaws and somewhere around the bend of the first block, I began to hear the theme from *Chariots of Fire* playing in my head.

This went on for about a week after which I began to run triathlons. Well, actually they were more like tri-ath-lawns—I would run past at least three lawns before collapsing. Then, as I lay on the asphalt gasping for air, Scott would jog in circles around me. It was fun for awhile—both of us being athletes and all. But soon, I was back to my books, finding it much more stimulating to read about exercise than actually do it.

Scott likes fruit desserts; I'm a chocolate-nut woman. He likes shoot-'em-up Westerns or cliff-hanger adventures. I like beautifully photographed British films where even the lips hardly move. He doesn't have a lazy bone in his body. When I relax (which is often), people wonder whether I have a bone in my body at all. He takes showers. I adore long, hot baths. And so it goes—tomato, tomahto, potato, potahto. But we can't call the whole thing off. We've got too much invested. Besides, as opposite as we are, we're getting awfully attached to each other.

It's also interesting to ponder the family traits we each brought into this marriage. Scott's folks are the hardworking, outgoing type—lots of family camping, ski trips, and so forth. Stoic, hearty stock.

My ancestors, on the other hand, might best be described as "Frills R Us." When we praise, it's with effusive gushing. When we laugh, it's the belly-shaking, knee-slapping sort. We're also a sensitive lot, so disappointments are expressed by throwing ourselves across the bed in heart-rending sobs. Writers, dancers, actors, and inventors populate our family tree.

When Scott and I came to the union of marriage, we brought traits with us that came from our parents and grandparents. But the really great thing about joining with another person in marriage—the thing that makes it such a mystery—is the way we purposely cleave to someone totally "other" than ourselves. We "marry" the flavors of our souls and spirits—by choice—into a marriage that is as unique as the two people who form it.

And when that marriage is aged and blended—not too much, but gently as with the slightest swirl of a spoon—mmmmmmm, it can be incredibly refreshing.

◆ ◆ ◆

I pray…that all of them may be one, Father, just as you are in me and I am in you.

JOHN 17: 20, 21

Marriage is an alliance entered into by a man who can't sleep with the windows shut, and a woman who can't sleep with the windows open.

—**George Bernard Shaw**

My Favorite Thoughts on Exercise

I had to give up jogging for my health. My thighs kept rubbing together and setting my panty hose on fire.

Amazing! You just hang something in your closet for a while, and it shrinks two sizes.

Inside some of us is a thin person struggling to get out, but she can usually be sedated with a few pieces of chocolate cake.

Part II

♦ ♦ ♦

Married Bliss– or Blitz?

Adjusting romantic expectations to reality

7

Wedding Wows

I write this in the month of June, a month full of fresh-faced brides and grooms eager to go straight from the chapel to Happily Ever After. But us old timers know all too well that "happily ever after" only happens in fairy tales. "Happily here and there," maybe. Or "more happily than not," per-haps. But nobody, except Cinderella and Sleeping Beauty, gets Happily Ever After *every* day.

Just the other day I met a young engaged couple, dressed like cowboy wedding cake toppers in look-alike jeans, boots, and western shirts. The young man, discovering that Scott and I had married at 17 and 18, asked me how to make a marriage last. In response, I decided to write a few "Real Life Vows for Bubba and His Bride"—revealing the sweat-shirt truth behind the tuxedo and white-lace vows.

> I, Bubba, take thee, Beautiful Bride, to be my lawfully wedded wife...
>
> *To have...* That is, when you aren't too tired from chasing kids all day or staying up all night with a

baby. Since quantity and quality ebb and flow, I'll try to go with the flow and not whine with the ebb. And I'll remember that sometimes the sexiest thing a man can do for a woman is listen and empathize.

And to hold...Even when everything in me screams, "Run fast—in the opposite direction!" Because no matter what's wrong, I know what you usually need when you're upset is to simply be held.

Being faithful only unto you...You will be it for me. The end of the line. But that's okay, because one real woman is all that I'll ever need. And I'll remember that to light your fire, I've got to strike the match early in the day.

In Sickness...I'll do my best to be helpful and sympathetic even when you have the kind of sickness involving disgusting unmentionables. Until I get the hang of it, I'll call your mom and ask what I should do with you.

And in health...It may be a challenge to stay healthy while you're learning to cook. But I can always run out for a salad. So I'll pretend I love burnt corn dog and popsicle dinners because I care about your feelings more than food.

For richer, for poorer...Realistically, we're probably looking at a good year wait on the "richer" stage. In the meantime, this may mean we're "sharing-a-small-cheeseburger-with-no-soft-drink-at-McDonald's" poor. And we can't run up credit cards or go home to Momma and Daddy every time the going gets tough. Together, we'll find a way to make it.

In good times...We'll have a lot of these, if we can just remember how to play and have fun together after we are "responsible married adults." We'll need to get away together when the stress builds up—even if it's just going for a walk under the stars. And these good times will be so sweet we'll forget about the rest of the world and its problems, at least for a while.

And in bad...Even when I wake up next to you one morning, and your make-up's gone and your thighs look as though they've got hail damage—I'll remember it's you I love and not the package outside. And when all the feeling disappears, I won't panic. I know these times will come, but I'll work at our marriage until the feelings come back—including going for "help" if neither of us knows what to do. (A marriage counselor? I'd rather be pecked to death by baby ducks, but for us, Babe, I'll do it.)

To love...I'll tell you "I love you" every day because women have a short memory in this category. And I'll remember that "Gee, you're more beautiful to me now than you've every been" equals at least three "I love you's." Sharing a private joke or a knowing wink across a crowded room may be worth ten "I love you's." And "I'm sorry" and "I forgive you" are equal to at least a hundred.

And to cherish...I'll remember that you need to be treated like a piece of fine china. This means I won't get out of the pick-up, walk toward the house, look back to see you still sitting there waiting, and say, "What's the matter, Sugar, your arm broke?"

From this day forward...Wow. From now to eternity. For this I'll need supernatural strength. When you turn your back to me at night, I'll hang in there because I know I'm accepted by a Savior who never fails me even when I turn my back to Him. And when I act like a jerk and fail at loving you, remember His love will never fail you either. And with the Lord guiding us, we get unlimited fresh starts.

Till death do us part...This means I'll never leave you a note telling you to "Get an attorney, it's over." This is the most binding contract we'll ever make, for we both know forever is a really, really long time. Someday we'll get old. And I want to be rocking next to you, holding love-weathered hands. Sweethearts, forever and always.

A word to young lovers out there: Just wait until you're middle-aged and know each other's faults, have weathered some major storms—and are still crazy in love. All I can say is that nothing we've ever worked to keep has been as well worth saving as our marriage.

◆ ◆ ◆

"This is it!" Adam exclaimed. "She is part of my own bone and flesh! Her name is 'woman' because she was taken out of a man." This explains why a man leaves his father and mother and is joined to his wife in such a way that the two become one person.

GENESIS 2:23,24 TLB

When two people are under the influence of the most violent, most insane, most delusive, and most transient of passions, they are required to swear that they will remain in that excited, abnormal, and exhausting condition continuously until death do them part.

—George Bernard Shaw

A Letter from an Old Newlywed

Dear Becky,

I first discovered your books the day before I got married. Since my college dorm had closed for the summer, I was staying at my mother's house and was enduring the longest period of family togetherness I had for quite sometime. Needing something to "take me away," I hit my mother's bookshelf. Her bookshelf was always full of books about real people that were peppered with humor and inspiration. As I looked over the rows of familiar titles, an author who was new to the shelf caught my eye. I reached for the copy of *Worms In My Tea* and read the first few pages....I was hooked.

For the next few hectic days, that book went everywhere with me—it was my escape. When we left for the honeymoon, there I was, book in tow. On the plane and on lazy afternoons in the sun, I took the opportunity to indulge in the zany tales of this woman from the piney woods. I remember reading about the crazy fights and other adventures you endured in the early years of your marriage. I even recall thinking in all of my newly-married wisdom that you and your husband were definitely insane—no two normal, well-adjusted people would ever find themselves in the crazy fights and situations you two had.

Now, three years of marriage later, I am hardly an expert on the topic but I have come to the realization that either you and Scott are completely normal, or we're all insane.

My husband and I have made it a habit of giving our newly married friends a "First Aid Kit" for their marriage that always includes one of your books about marriage. The card we attach explains each item in the kit and ends with an explanation that the book is "for those times when you think your marriage is absolutely crazy and you're not certain that it's exactly what you signed up for," and instructs the newly-weds to "read this and remember you are completely normal (or else we're all crazy)!"

8

There Is a Season

It was a gorgeous morning as I sat alone enjoying a French pastry and a cup of cappuccino in one of the most beautiful hotels in America. What more could a woman ask for? Every so often, God lets me experience a little taste of heaven—and being alone with a pastry and good coffee is about as close as it gets. As I nibbled and sipped, I let my Bible fall open onto the table. Sunlight from the skylight overhead illuminated a familiar passage from Ecclesiastes. "There is a time for everything, and a season for every activity under heaven" (Ecclesiastes 3:1).

As I sat basking in God's presence that lovely, unhurried morning, it dawned on me that if a marriage is to grow strong and full—like a bountiful oak tree—it must go through its own times and seasons. For example, in marriage there is...

> *A time to be born...*A season of Eden-like love—the idealized, wonderfully romantic time when our affections for each other are as fresh as a newborn baby.

55

And a time to die...There also comes a time to die to our unrealistic fantasies, such as having, or being, the perfect mate. This *necessary loss* that author Judith Viorst described has to occur before mature love can begin.

A time to plant...As love matures, most couples begin to put down roots, make a home, and begin a family. There comes a season of settling down.

A time to uproot...Then just as the young family gets settled, a notice arrives, signaling it's time to start all over. Move, start a new job, face new challenges. Yet, these times of uprooting and re-settling can even be adventurous, producing a "you and me against the world" kind of feeling in a marriage.

A time to kill...No, not each other. (Though there may be times we're tempted!) There comes a season of reflection when we ask God to destroy sinful patterns that have crept into our marriages. Proverbs 27:17 says, "As iron sharpens iron, so one man sharpens another." One reason God places us together is to unveil each other's blind spots—self-defeating and harmful ways of reacting. This season is perhaps the most painful of all—it gets awfully hot when iron is at the task of sharpening iron.

A time to heal...After having gone through the refining fire of brokeness, couples need a season of healing, a time to cool off and comfort one another. Think of it as becoming each other's Aloe Vera.

A time to tear down...Occasionally, Scott has had to help me tear down a wall of pride or self importance. This guy who knows me best calls me on those pesky, subtle sins that others let me get away with.

A time to build...On the other hand, when my self-esteem has been bruised by the world, my husband is the one I want at my side to make it all better again. He builds me up.

A time to weep...I'm not sure a couple can fully understand the concept of "becoming one" until they've wept together in a time of deep sorrow.

A time to laugh...It also helps becoming one to laugh so hard they fall off the bed and onto the floor together.

A time to mourn...During those days of numbing sadness, after the weeping, the best gift you have to offer each other is a hand to hold and a shoulder to lean on.

A time to dance...These are the seasons of festivity, when the pleasure of being old people in love bubbles up and overflows—when a husband spontaneously invites his wife into his arms for a spin around the kitchen floor, just for the fun of it.

A time to embrace...I'm looking at a black and white picture of a man swirling a woman around in the kind of embrace you see in old movies, usually at train stations. These are Home-Sweet-Home times: moments of reuniting at the end of an absence or simply at the end of a long day.

A time to refrain from embracing...This can be a healthy and necessary part of growing in love. Not only do we need times of solitude for personal reflection, but it's often in the lonely times that God reminds us why we need each other after all.

A time to keep...There are special moments in marriage we want to freeze in time, to treasure in the memory bank of our mind—births of our children, anniversaries, walks by the sea.

A time to throw away...Then there are those memories we need to toss. We all have to periodically toss the garbage of grudges into the bin of forgiveness.

A time to be silent...That's right—silent. We forgo our own agenda to focus on our mate—listening without judgment, without hurrying, listening below the surface of words for the feelings underneath. Giving our spouses focused attention is a rare and precious treasure.

A time to speak...Then comes the time to speak up. Yes, sometimes we have to speak in confrontation. But more often may it be "I love you," "I'm sorry," or "You're precious to me" that leaves our lips and enters into our loved one's ears.

A time for war...Fights and disagreements will come, so we don't need to be terrified when they happen. Though painful, an argument can clear the air and allow for a new start. To disagree and argue are parts of what it means to be a human being.

A time for peace...Would we really appreciate peacetime if we'd not survived a few marital battles? I love the delicious relief, the joy of everything being okay between us again. Ah...peace—a season to savor.

Just as spring follows winter, so the most enjoyable seasons of marriage come after a time of bitter coldness. That's why it's important to remember that one season does not a marriage make. Hang on through the winter, for things have a way of blossoming again.

◆ ◆ ◆

He has made everything beautiful in its time.

ECCLESIASTES 3:11

*If men and wimmen think they
are marrin' angels, they'll find
out they'll have to settle down
and keep house with human critters.
I never seen a year yet, that didn't have
more or less winter in it.*

—Josiah Allens' wife

9

Sea-crets of Contentment

It was Scott's birthday and the first year I'd actually made a profit from my writing. So I splurged, reserving a beach house for a sun-splashed week in Gulf Shores, Alabama. My husband is a sea-loving man: loves salt in the air, sun on his back, dolphins leaping the blue-green waves. How we both anticipated long, lazy days of nothing but sunshine.

Neither of us was emotionally prepared for seven long, lazy days of nonstop rain.

In my whole life, I do not remember it raining for seven days straight—not anywhere, any time, or for any reason. Why did this have to happen during our one precious week of vacation? Each day I would walk out on the sun deck to watch a new storm gathering. "Oh, Lord," I'd whine with the fervency of a child begging for candy. "Please, just a bit of blue. Just a shimmer of sun. Please, God, PLEASE. I'll be a good girl, really I will." Then with a clap of thunder, I'd get my unwanted answer. "Not today, child, not today."

"But Father," I'd continue, "this was supposed to be our ROMANTIC getaway! Two married lovers lounging in sun-drenched bliss. This week is turning out wrong, all wrong!" As I fell asleep to the sound of rain on the roof each night, I couldn't help thinking of John Lennon's famous line, "Life is what happens to you while you're making other plans."

I often hear the same sort of lament about marriage that I felt about the weather that week.

"Becky, this marriage is not what I signed up for. Where are the blue skies? The birds tweeting happily in the background?"

In truth, most of us naïvely said "I do" expecting unending days of sunshine, not weeks of nonstop rain. So what can we do when our fantasy vacation, or dream marriage, is rained out by reality?

Of all the choices we could make, only a few yield long-term contentment. The older I get, the more I'm convinced that marriage is God's invitation to cross the threshold from childishness to maturity. As one man wisely said, "Marriage is our last best chance to grow up."

One of the grown-up ways we can react when the postcard picture doesn't match the real scene is to mentally adjust our vision. We can learn to love the rain. Or to quote a line from a famous '60s song, "Honey, love the one you're with."

Put your energies into loving the life you've got. If you don't have the sunshine you signed up for, Honey, get an umbrella and learn to love walks in the rain. Your spouse was not what you imagined? Then learn to appreciate the one you married.

One afternoon during our vacation the rain finally let up, but the sun had still not shown its bright face. Scott found me sitting in overcast silence on the deck and took my hand.

"Let's go for a drive," he said. "I want to show you something."

We drove for awhile, then parked the car near an uninhabited strip of beach. The colors along the oceanside were not what I'd pictured when I'd planned our get-away. There was no bright blue sky, no white fluffy clouds, no sparkling white sand against aqua waves.

But suddenly it struck me how beautiful the beach was. Without the glare of the sun, the ocean, sand, and sky were soft, varying shades of earthy tones: subtle taupes, soft beiges, and restful tan. A light mist gave an ethereal look to the seascape. I could almost hear God whisper, *"I'm here, Becky. But today I'm offering this kind of beauty. Can't you appreciate what I've painted for you here? Now?"*

Smiling, I reached to pick up a pink seashell just as Scott ran over with a huge starfish, anxious to share his find. We felt suddenly young, like two kids at play—me in my overalls rolled up to my knees, Scott in his T-shirt and jeans. For the next hour, we walked and ran up and down the beach, gathering treasures and shouting, "Look at this one!" or "See what I found!"

Before long, we felt droplets of rain on our shoulders. But this time I didn't complain. For how many opportunities do you get to walk in the rain with the one you love, hand in hand, pockets bulging with seashell riches?

It's all a matter of perspective. Sometimes the sun shines from the outside in, sometimes it has to come from the inside out.

◆ ◆ ◆

Even the darkness will not be dark to you; the night will shine like the day, for darkness is as light to you.

PSALM 139:12

We come to love not by finding a perfect person, but by learning to see an imperfect person perfectly.

—**Anonymous**

10

How to Be
an In-Law

The first year Scott and I were married we were not only newlyweds, we were teenagers. I had just celebrated my seventeenth birthday and, only one month before, Scott had turned the wise old age of eighteen. We brought into our marriage all the maturity of a girl who was still afraid of the dark, and a boy who shaved his fuzz once every two weeks. As you might imagine, it didn't take us kids long to get into a fuss once our honeymoon ended.

Soon after we married, Scott and I took a job cleaning a church and nearby Christian school to help support ourselves and pay for the full-time load of college courses we were both taking. I wasn't prepared for the transformation Scott went through, from loving husband to—the boss—MY boss. It seemed to me that Scott took special pleasure in coming up behind me and offering unsolicited critique.

"Becky," he'd point out, "you left a little smear mark on the water fountain spigot."

In mock horror, I'd reply, "No! How could I have possibly left that pea-sized area of chrome un-waxed? There's no telling what evil could befall us if we drink out of a smeared spigot!"

My response did not go over well. As a matter of fact, it only served to force my young husband to take an even *more* Gestapo-like approach.

"What are you doing?" he once asked as he swung open a door to the empty classroom I'd been cleaning. I was caught—vacuum handed, vacuuming the way *I* liked to do it—pushing the vacuum cleaner in and out around me, like rays pointing out from the sun.

"This looks just awful," Scott scolded as he pried the vacuum from my determined hands and began pushing the machine across the room. "You're supposed to vacuum in perfectly straight parallel lines, back and forth across the carpet, like so."

That did it. On my way out, I spun around and said, "Guess what? I quit! And please take note: I'll be walking in a perfectly straight line—all of the way out of the building."

I marched out of the church and into the August sunshine, then began the five-mile trek toward the house of my childhood.

I'll go back to my Home Sweet Home, I thought, the anger now rising into fury, *back where my mother and father think everything I do is cute and adorable.* I couldn't wait to tell my mother what a dictator I'd mistakenly married. I could hear her comforting, motherly words as she'd rush to take my side. By the time I arrived at my parents' front door, I was wilting from heat, parched with thirst, and ready to explode.

"What happened?" Mother asked in concern as she ushered me into the kitchen and poured me a tall glass of water.

My thirst quenched, I found my voice and began to tell my mother in no uncertain terms how I'd married a perfectionist nut. Then I sat waiting expectantly for her outpouring of sympathy, my pitiful head resting dramatically on my hands. What I got instead was a chuckle! My own mother actually found this whole situation amusing.

"Oh, Becky," she laughed again as she spoke, "you two will work it out. All couples have to." And that was, basically, that.

From the day each of my siblings and I married, our parents embraced our spouses as if they were their own. They took no sides, except the side of "Marriage isn't easy—but it's worth the trouble. And it's forever." Whenever we landed at their doorstep with complaints, we received just enough sympathy to let us know we were loved, promises of their prayers, and a gentle push back in the direction of our spouses. They had complete confidence in our ability to work it out, either alone or with the aid of an unbiased counselor. (Scott's parents, I might add, held the exact same stance. I wonder if our folks conspired to hold a united front on this before we married?)

I had an opportunity to meet my parents for a cup of coffee at an outdoor cafe recently. As we reminisced and shared, I looked at them and said, "You know what? You two should write a book called *How To Be Great In-Laws*. The two of you refused to take sides when we kids and our mates disagreed. Instead you emphasized your love for us AND our mates. I think you played a tremendous part in keeping our "Marriage 9-1-1" times from turning into marital fatalities."

Mother's eyes glistened with tears. "Thank you, Honey," she replied warmly, reaching out to touch my outstretched arm. "We just love our kids, that's all."

And I knew when she said "our kids," she meant not only me, my brother, David, and my sister, Rachel. "Our kids" included her two sons-in-law (both named Scott) and Barb, her daughter-in-law.

I pray that when my children, Zach, Zeke, Rachel, and Gabriel, marry, I'll determine from the start to view my daughters-in-law and son-in-law as daughters and son-in-*love*. That I'll find a way to pass on the confidence our parents and grandparents passed on to us—that most things in life, including rocky relationships, have a way of resolving themselves if you just get back in the ring with a fresh perspective and cooler heads. Then keep praying, trying, learning, and experimenting until you find a way to live Happily Ever After—at least every now and then.

◆ ◆ ◆

I have told you this so that my joy may be in you and that your joy may be complete.... Love each other as I have loved you.

JOHN 15:11, 12

The course of true love never did run smooth.

—**William Shakespeare**

Part III

◆ ◆ ◆

Is There Sex
After Marriage?

Keeping romance sizzling at home,
avoiding temptations "out there"

11

How to Handle a Woman

My editor at *Home Life,* Jon Walker, received the following from a lieutenant in the Navy who was deployed aboard ship.

> PLEASE PRAY
>
> I'm married to a wonderful woman and she has been making sacrifice after sacrifice while I go out to sea for the U.S. Navy.
>
> This current separation is testing our faith in the Lord and we are stumbling.
>
> Please pray for us. Her mother just sent me a copy of the July issue of *Home Life* and it's been a hit onboard the ship, particularly the "Marriage 911" piece on "How to Really Love a Woman."

I can't tell you how thrilled I was to think about a bunch of tough sailors at sea concerned about how to be better husbands. It is with great pleasure, I share that column again.

Men should know that women sometimes get together and play a game called "Let's Compare Husbands." It's a lot like a card game, actually. And, as with face cards, not all hubby's personality traits have equal value. According to the rule book, having the correct combinations is also important. I've played a few rounds myself and have had some pretty stiff competition, but usually I'm assured of having at least one ace in the hole. This is the way it goes.

"All right, girls," Player Number One says, "I'm holding a man who picks up his own socks and knows how to whip up a box of macaroni and cheese by himself."

"Wow," replies Player Number Two. "That's hard to beat. But I'll raise you. My husband can unstop a backed-up commode and doesn't mind changing the cat box."

"Oh, you're kidding!" says Player Number Three. "You've got a man with a strong stomach? All I've got is a regular paycheck coming in, a great father to the kids, and no snoring at night."

"Well, ladies," I say as I lay down my cards with a flourish. "Read 'em and weep. I've got a husband who's stubborn, knows how to say just the wrong thing at just the wrong time, and has the patience of a gnat. But when he's good, he's very, very good. He's tender. He's playful. And girls, I'm sorry to have to tell you this, but—he's also romantic."

"Oh, pooh!" the rest lament. "It's not fair—Becky's holding the King of Hearts again!"

I may be slightly overstating the case, but I haven't yet met a woman who wouldn't trade neatness and steadiness for a man who enjoys candlelight dinners, interesting conversations, and is known to, on occasion, waltz his wife across the kitchen floor.

I know there are many men out there who think romantic equals softness equals big sissy. Most of these men, unfortunately, are dateless, divorced, or sleeping on the couch. Take it from me—the surest way to a woman's heart is the most direct route. Go straight for the heart.

When I think of romance and tenderness in our relationship, I think of the countless little things that add to our love. The way our bodies "spoon" together when we snuggle close at night. The way we sometimes talk to each other like little kids just because it's fun. When Scott completes a special project on the house, he may come grab my hand and in a boyish voice urge, "Come see my big roof!"

I love the way Scott supports my crazy endeavors: from singing to teaching to catering to writing to one wild attempt at starting a Paper Hair Bow business (Don't even ask). I like the perpetual conversation we have going, the nuances of familiarity: baby talk, pet names and phrases. The meals we've shared in greasy cafés and romantic candlelit restaurants.

I love the way Scott graciously reads my work while allowing me to stare at him, taking note of every twitch, every minuscule response. By some miracle, he's able to completely tune out the fact that my face is five inches away from his. He just pencils his critique as if I'm invisible. Then he always tells me the truth—where the manuscript made him laugh, where it touched him, where he had no idea what on earth I was trying to say. Once the writing project is a wrap, I can always count on one thing: He will be prouder of me than any other human being on the face of the earth.

But most of all, I've enjoyed the slow dances to old love songs pouring from the kitchen radio.

I like this man. Very much.

Madeleine L'Engle penned the tender love story of her marriage to Hugh Franklin in the book, *Two-Part Invention: The Story of a Marriage*. Near the end of the story, there's a heartbreaking scene where Madeleine is holding her husband in her arms as he takes his last breath. She was unable, for several moments, to release her embrace. At one point, she turned to the attending physician and said, "It is hard to let go beloved flesh." Madeleine finished the book with a beautiful line from a poem by Conrad Aiken, a poem Hugh had read to her some forty years earlier on the night he proposed marriage:

> *Music I heard with you was more than music,*
> *And bread I broke with you was more than bread.*

I cannot read those words without thinking of Scott, and I cannot think long on them without tears coming to my eyes. For one day, I, too, may have to "let go beloved flesh." And when I do, it will be my husband's tender, romantic expressions that I'll surely miss the most. No, moments like that don't happen all the time, but when they do, they make even everyday "bread and music" extraordinary.

◆ ◆ ◆

Rejoice with the wife of your youth and always be enraptured with her love.

PROVERBS 5:18,19

Chains do not hold a marriage together. It is threads, hundreds of tiny threads, which sew people together through the years.

—Simone Signoret

Kara Oh has written a book for women called *Men Made Easy*, but the best part is at the back of the volume, where she wrote a mini pull-out book for men (knowing a man's nature for "just the facts, ma'am"). She shares "How to Make Her Happy" via the following twelve secrets.

- *Romance is the key to sex.* (Remember all those romantic things you did to win her in the first place? Keep doing them now.)

- *For her, sex takes time.* (Rent the movie Don Juan deMarco and listen how he talks about women and making love—then adopt that mindset with the one woman in your life.)

- *Talking is the way she connects with you.* All you have to do is look at her and pay attention when she talks; she'll think she's died and gone to heaven. It's that important to her, and that simple.

- *She needs to hear you say you care.* For her to really FEEL your love, she needs to hear the words.

- *She needs to hear she's attractive.* Women get unsure about how they look—it's our culture. So, tell her regularly that she's beautiful and sexy.

- *Her feelings need to be honored.* Never tell her to not feel her emotions. A sure-fire winner: Ask her, "What are you feeling?" Then sit down and listen.

- *Making up is hard to do.* Most women tend to let everything spill out. Do your best to pay attention, let her vent, but don't let all the words get to you. She doesn't mean a lot of what she says when she's upset. The more conciliatory you are ("I was being a jerk" and that sort of thing) the more she'll be stopped in her tracks.

- *She likes to be pampered.* Remember: give her gifts of personal luxury—a romantic dinner, a day at the spa. Changing the oil in the car is nice, but it isn't personal enough.

- *She needs your respect*: Treat her like a lady at all times, and she'll treat you with the respect that you enjoy.

- *She needs to feel secure.* What really helps is ongoing affection: Hold her hand, hug her, touch her in gentle and reassuring ways.

- *She needs your time and attention*: Set aside time now and then to focus just on her. The rewards will far outweigh the effort.

- *She wants a man who makes her feel like a woman*. Be masculine, but do it with sensuality and sensitivity. (Ignore the militant feminist movement. It did a lot of damage to romance. Yes, open the car door, carry heavy things for her, pull out her chair.)

12

Viagra Falls

You can't pick up a newspaper or magazine these days that doesn't have some article about Viagra or yohimbe or ginseng or ginkgo or some other new herb or drug guaranteed to stimulate libido.

"The world seems to be flooded with news about men and their interest in sex," I remarked to my friend Brenda Waggoner during our weekly lunch of Chinese chicken salad at Applebees. "What IS it about men and sex, anyway? Why is it so important to them?"

Brenda is not only one of my dearest friends, she's also a professional family counselor. By nature of her profession, she's unflappable and honest. The kind of friend you can ask about sex—over salad—without her missing a beat. Brenda also relishes life: everything from a cool breeze to hot coffee to warm conversation can cause her to pause and comment on God's goodness. I was soon to discover she had the same fresh outlook on lovemaking in marriage.

"You know, Becky," Brenda paused to take a sip of water, then smiled. "I don't think most women have any idea how healing sex is to a man. Maybe if women knew and appreciated how men use this wordless, sensual language of love, they might enjoy sex more."

"So," I thought aloud, "are you saying that what an afternoon of shopping and coffee and chocolate and conversation do for a woman, 30 minutes of passion can do for a man?"

Brenda laughed. "Yep. Most men feel they can't match their wives in the verbal arena. Lots of men give up even trying to engage in meaningful conversation after a few years of defeat. Yet, men long to please their wives, to see them happy, to show their love. And sex, to them, feels like the most natural way to do that."

"I've noticed that with my husband," I answered thoughtfully. "And sex also seems to be the way he gets his emotional cup filled back up after the world has punctured his ego or drained his energy."

"Isn't that the truth?" Brenda nodded in agreement. "Nothing makes a man feel more loved and ready to take on the world than spending some unhurried, fun, intimate time with his wife."

I drove from lunch that afternoon with a fresh perspective and renewed desire to keep the sensual spark alive in our soon-to-be-over-the-hill marriage. Brenda had reminded me that sex is a God-given balm, a heaven-sent gift for our bodies and souls.

Spying a superstore on the way home, I pulled in and bought some musk-scented candles and a black nightie. What could it hurt?

After all, if sex was my man's language, I intended to do everything within my power to stay fluent.

◆ ◆ ◆

May your fountain be blessed, and may you rejoice in the wife of your youth. A loving doe, a graceful deer—may her breasts satisfy you always, may you ever be captivated by her love.

PROVERBS 5:18, 20

Seems to me the basic conflict between men and women, sexually, is that men are like firemen. To us, sex is an emergency, and no matter what we're doing we can be ready in two minutes. Women, on the other hand, are like fire. They're very exciting, but the conditions have to be exactly right for it to occur.

—Jerry Seinfeld

Light Her Fire

Remember that fatigue is probably the Number 1 romance killer for most women. If you have young babies or children, give your wife an evening break or afternoon nap when you're feeling amorous. A little morning hint or daytime phone call letting her know you're in the mood for love helps her begin the all-important simmering process. Most women like a little time to mentally shift gears from Mommy or Career Woman or Homemaker or Bible Study Leader to Lover.

Compliment your wife's body. A woman needs to feel sexy and pretty in order to respond to her husband's advances. She doesn't want to feel like your "most available legal outlet." She wants to know she's your special lady, your lover, your first and forever choice. Your verbal compliments on her appearance will go a long way toward increasing her desire for lovemaking. (Just take a look at the Song of Solomon for affirmation of this!)

13

We're Just Friends
(Warning! Warning! Warning!)

I received many poignant letters as a result of the following column. One woman came up to me at a retreat, asked if we could visit privately, and with tears in her eyes, she reached into her purse and unfolded a worn copy of this column.

"I've been carrying it around with me," she began. "I found myself having feelings for a very empathetic, handsome man who has made overtures to me. But I love my husband and children. Every time I feel the pull of temptation, I pull out this column and re-read it. It has literally been my emotional lifesaver these past several months.

I was lunching with a young woman who could have been the poster woman for the Good Girl Christian: wonderful wife, loving mother, flower print dress, lace collar, Bible in her purse. As she relaxed with me, she confessed there had been a time when she was terribly tempted to have an affair with a man she worked with in a Christian business. "I wasn't in the Word like I should have been at the time," she began to explain, in shame.

I looked at her and in all sincerity said, "You know what? Even if you had been reading your Bible every hour, you may still have felt attracted. Feeling drawn to the opposite sex—especially to someone who affirms your worth—is as natural as breathing. It's not a sin to feel attracted. It's what happens next that matters."

Just hearing that feeling attracted to someone other than your mate, isn't a sin, brought her relief. This sort of crazy emotional crush happens to nearly everyone at one time or another! Ask almost any older man or woman and they'll tell you, "I've been there." "But," we ask, "how can I possibly be a Christian, a happily married person and feel attracted to someone else?" Because, as my friend Bill Gillham says, "Our earthsuits were designed to want love." And our "feeler," as Bill calls it, doesn't discriminate who that love comes from. Our will has to grow up and make wise choices, even though our "feeler" may be throwing a carnal fit.

So what does a woman do when she feels herself day-dreaming about a man who's not her husband? What does a husband do when he finds himself wandering by a woman's desk more often than he should because she looks great or smells good or makes him laugh and feel special? Here's my best girlfriend advice:

- *Run to a trusted friend or counselor* and tell them honestly what's going on in your mind. Once the monster is out of the closet, it almost immediately shrinks in size.

The Lord promises to provide a way out of temptation. The biggest escape hatch opens as soon as you realize you may be walking into trouble. The longer you wait to get help, the harder it will be to escape the web.

- *Back off from any relationship that drains energy from your marriage.*

A Christian counselor once told Scott and me that we needed to begin our marriage counseling by backing off from close friendships of the opposite sex. He explained that these friendships were draining vital energy. "And," he said, "you two are going to need every ounce of your emotional energy for the task ahead."

It proved to be some of the best advice we've ever received.

- *See through the lie of an affair.*

In the movie *The Age of Innocence*, the main character falls in love with a married man, but refuses to give in to her feelings, asking him a poignant question. "How can we find happiness behind the backs of those who trust us?"

What a needed splash of cold water! An affair may bring temporary excitement, but it will never bring lasting happiness. How can we be happy behind the backs of those who trust us?

Today our marriage is much, much stronger—and yes, both of us enjoy warm friendships with people of both sexes. I love and appreciate a great number of good men. I think God did a *wonderful* thing when he created them, and I enjoy their company immensely. But I enjoy friendships with them within careful boundaries. Scott and I go out as couples with other couples, a great way to relate to opposite sex friends without the high risk of friendship turning into attraction. I've learned the wisdom of keeping my professional and personal friendships with other men light and upbeat. I look to my husband or girlfriends when I need a shoulder to cry on.

I never talk to another man about the intimate details of a struggle in my marriage, unless he's a counselor or trusted pastor. (I know too many "just friends" situations, and have stacks of tear-stained mail from readers who write, "It all started so innocently. I told this guy friend how my husband wasn't meeting my needs, and the next thing I knew, he was offering to meet them instead.")

If Scott's emotionally unavailable and I need to unload and get feedback, I have "lunch therapy" with two close trusted female friends (and know I can always telephone my funny, compassionate sister as well). These women are pro-marriage and have good-hearted senses of humor. Though they listen with appropriate empathy, when I ask advice, they always point me to Christ.

I also limit my most time-consuming friendships, the ones where I share often and deeply from my heart, to my husband first, and then to other women. I put lots of time and energy into my marriage and treasure my female friendships. With all this energy going out in positive directions, I laugh and empathize with Erma Bombeck's famous line, "I'm just too tired for an affair!"

And, besides, nothing feels as good as falling in love, again and again, with the same man.

◆ ◆ ◆

My son, pay attention to my wisdom, listen
well to my words of insight....For the lips of
an adulteress drip honey, and her speech is
smoother than oil; but in the end she is bitter
as gall, sharp as a doubled-edged sword.

PROVERBS 5:1,3,4

*It is absurd to pretend that one
cannot love the same woman
always, as to pretend that a good
artist needs several violins to
execute a piece of music.*

—Balzac

Recipe for an Affair

When an affair starts, it begins as a friendship. You share problems with the other
person, and that person shares problems
with you. Usually, for the affair to blossom,
you have to see this other person quite
often: every day at work or frequently
through a friendship, being on a
committee or board, or some other
responsibility that brings you together.

As your friendship deepens, you start
giving each other mutual support and
encouragement, especially in regard to
your unmet needs. Life is difficult. Many
people become extremely disillusioned
about their lives. When they find someone
encouraging and supportive, the
attraction toward that person acts as a
powerful magnet. Sooner or later, you find
yourself in bed with your encouraging
and supportive friend. It just seems to
"happen." You don't intend it, and neither
does your friend.[1]

—Dr. Willard F. Harley

14

Love Lessons from a Child

Valentine's Day. That lovey-dovey time of year. Time for heart-shaped boxes filled with luscious chocolates that turn women's bodies into heart-shaped balloons. Time for pink teddy bears, long-stemmed roses, love letters and romantic cards. It's enough to make everyone a little nervous.

I'll never forget the card Scott gave me on our first "married" Valentine's Day. It would have been lovely, sentimental, and touching. Except that he signed it, "Love, Scott Freeman."

As a young bride of 17, I was crushed. *How could Scott make a joke of this, our first Valentine's Day as man and wife?* As a young groom of 18, Scott was equally mortified. *How in the world could I have messed up so badly, accidentally signing my first and last name?* he thought. Unfortunately, it would not be the first Valentine's Day that ended with the two of us sleeping back to back in silence. We could have taken a lesson from a seven-year-old.

A few years ago, our youngest child, Gabe, was struck by Cupid with full force. I mean the arrow hit him straight in the heart. One day around mid-February, I happened upon a couple of notes Gabe had penned to his new little love. Its heartfelt sincerity was palpable.

> I love you more than dimmines. Yur more preshus than baby Jesus lyin in a manjer with sheperds watching over.
>
> love, Gabe
> P.S. its all true

Gabe decided to give his new girl the best present his savings could buy. So he gathered up all his dollars, quarters, dimes, and pennies and bought a big fluffy white teddy bear. His sweetheart loved it and wrote to tell him so. Gabe was so touched he wrote her the following note, which I found a few days later typed on the computer.

> I'm glad you liked you're teddeybear. I rote a rime for you it goe'es like this
>
> I think you'r grandey
> I think you'r handey & I like to give canddey.
>
> I know it's short but you know I love you & that's all that matter's.
>
> love,
> Gabe

Oh, for the heart of a child. After a few years, and a few experiences of rejection, we grown-ups learn to temper our expressions of love. But not so with kids. They just lay it right out there, don't they? Their blunt tenderness is refreshing, reminding me not to guard my feelings of love quite so carefully. Especially around this sentimental time of year when it's a little more acceptable, even for adults, to go around wearing our hearts on our sleeves.

That special Valentine year, Gabe came home with a folder stuffed with school worksheets, coloring pages, dime-store cards, and boxes of hard candy hearts with deep, meaningful messages on them like, "Be mine." But there among the papers, I found yet another gem. Apparently Gabe's teacher had given the class a special Valentine's Day assignment, and Gabe, in his matter-of-fact manner, complied.

> I'm polst to tell you good things about Valentims. They are giving presents becouse it's fun to watch them open it. I usually give my friends stufft bears & chocklets. The party's are fun becouse we get cookies, candy, Sprite, & I can be with my friends. I just flat out like Vallintines.

I can't help myself. It's just flat out hard not to smile when you've got a sugar-lovin', tender-hearted kid around the house to remind you what life and love are all about.

P.S. to Reader: *I know this chapter's kinda short, but you know I love you—and hey, that's all that matters.*

◆ ◆ ◆

There is no fear in love. Perfect love drives out fear.

1 JOHN 4:18

There is only one happiness in life, to love and be loved.

—George Sand

Redneck Ode to a Valentine's Day

Kudzu is green,
My dog's name is Blue.
And I'm so lucky,
To have a sweet thang like you.

Yore hair is like cornsilk
A-flapping in the breeze.
Softer than Blue's,
And without all them fleas.

You move like the bass,
Which thrill me in May.
You ain't got no scales,
But I luv you anyway.

You have all yore teeth,
For which I am proud;
I hold my head high,
When we're in a crowd.

Like a good roll of duct tape
Yo're there fer yore man,
To patch up life's troubles,
And stick 'em in the can.

Yo're as strong as a four-wheeler
Racin' through the mud,
Yet fragile as that sanger,
Named Naomi Judd.

Yo're as cute as a junebug,
A-buzzin' overhead.
You ain't mean like no far ant,
Upon which I oft' tread.

When you hold me real tight,
Like a padded gunrack,
My life is complete;
Ain't nuttin' I lack.

And when you get old,
Like a '57 Chevy,
Won't put you on blocks,
And let grass grow up heavy.

Me 'n' you's like a Moon Pie,
With a RC cold drank,
We go together,
Like a skunk goes with stank.

Some men, they buy chocolate,
For Valentine's Day;
They git it at Wal-Mart,
It's romantic that way.

Some men git roses,
On that special day,
From the cooler at Kroger.
"That's impressive," I say.
Some men buy fine diamonds,
From a flea market booth.

"Diamonds are forever,"
They explain, suave and couth.

But for this man, honey,
These will not do.
For you are too special,
You sweet thang you.

I got you a gift,
Without taste nor odor,
Better than diamonds
it's a new trollin' motor.

—Anonymous

15

Window Dressing

The following story, adapted from my book *Marriage 9-1-1,* has been far and away the most requested "tell it again!" tale I've ever told. And, as my son Gabe is prone to say, "It's all true!"

I'm not, by any stretch of the imagination, what you would call a naturally wild woman. But I'd been married fifteen years, and felt our marriage needed a little chili pepper in the bedroom.

It all began with a romantic suggestion I gleaned from a book, *Light IIis Fire.* The author, Ellen Kriedman, suggests that wives use their ingenuity to come up with imaginative ways to have fun seducing their mate. The book assured me that, done properly, this technique should fire up the I-feel-a-chill-in-the air times most couples experience at some point in their relationship.

Nothing new here, really. Ever since the days when perky Mrs. Marabel Morgan first suggested we Christian women greet our husbands at the door dressed in plastic wrap and/or apron, we wives have spent a couple of decades trying to be the Total Woman. (Which, in reality, left many of us feeling more liked Totaled Women.) Still, I was game for anything to charge up the waning batteries of our love life.

And so, one night, as I was in this "Light His Fire/Total Woman" state of mind, I stepped out of the shower wrapped in a towel. Just then, I spied the lights of Scott's pickup truck in the driveway of our remote country home. Suddenly I could almost hear Dr. Kriedman whispering in my ear. *Why not? After all, you're married to the guy. Be playful! Be sexy! Have some fun with your man!*

So I dropped the towel and stood there in front of the window wearing nothing but my most seductive smile.

A few seconds later, there was a knock at the bedroom door. It was Scott. He opened the door a few hesitant inches and said, as calmly as possible, "Hi, Hon! I'm home! And guess what? GARY is with me."

My screams, I'm sure, awakened every possum and raccoon in nearby trees. I thought I would die. My thoughts were frenzied. *I've just flashed my best friend's husband!* I silently vowed to avoid Gary for the rest of my life. How could I face him without dissolving into a puddle of shame and embarrassment?

The next morning, Mary, Gary's wife, called bright and early.

"Becky," she said brightly, "Gary asked me to deliver a message to you." Switching to a deep French accent, she continued, "He says to tell you, 'Becky, jou look marvahlous.'"

When the laughter finally subsided on her end of the line, Mary added, "Hey, Becky, don't worry. He's been feeling a little down lately and this probably made his week."

Because they both had a great sense of humor, we all recovered fairly quickly. With understanding and the passing of years, I'm now able to hold a normal conversation with Gary without benefit of a paper bag over my head.

Needless to say, I'm much more careful with my "creative displays of affection" these days, but I still look for open opportunities to spice up our love life.

Sometimes, I leave short, sexy "song messages" on my husband's voice mail at work. "I just called to say I love you." "Unforgettable, that's what you are..." Women are resourceful. Once we put our minds to it, we can think of dozens of ways to "gift" our men.

My friend Brenda (the therapist) told me about receiving a box of scarves in the mail one sunny afternoon. They were meant to be props in a drama. However, as she felt their silkiness and relished the brilliant colors, she suddenly had a wild idea. Her husband was out mowing the yard. To his delight and amazement, when he looked up from the tractor, there was his lovely wife beckoning from the patio dressed in nothing but scarves tied around her. Needless to say, the lawn had to wait.

Sometimes we can even turn inconveniences into opportunities. I once had a flat tire in front of a hotel about an hour and a half from our home. I called Scott and said, "If you'll come fix my tire for me, I promise to make it worth your while." Then I asked the hotel clerk if there was a half-day rate for a room, explaining I needed a little time to take a nap, and study quietly, but would not be staying overnight. Sure enough, there was a nice day rate, and when Scott arrived and finished fixing the tire, he was both shocked and pleasantly surprised to discover I'd rented a room where we could freshen up, rest, and enjoy a long, leisurely "nap."

Every marriage gets predictable at times, where the bedroom seems more like a bored room. With a little spontaneous ingenuity, however, we can add some chili pepper to our love. After all, variety is the spice of life.

Just make completely sure that the coast is clear before you begin sprinkling your spice.

◆ ◆ ◆

Take me away with you—let us hurry! Let the King bring me into his chambers.

Song of Solomon 1:4

Truly, a little love-making is a very pleasant thing.

—L.E. Landon

Part IV

◆ ◆ ◆

Building Bridges over Troubled Valleys

Handling crises—big and small

16

Pre-Monster Syndrome

When Gabe was in first grade, he came home one day complaining about the boy who sat next to him in school.

"Mom," he moaned, "this is the whiniest kid. I mean, nobody can do anything to make him happy! All he does is gripe, gripe, gripe—all day long! Really, he's got the worst case of PMS I've ever seen in a kid."

Obviously, Gabriel knew that whatever PMS meant, it was bad but he didn't quite have all the details worked out. I struggled to keep a straight face and informed Gabriel that boys do not get PMS. His father decided it was time for a man-to-man talk.

"Son," he told him, "don't worry about trying to understand women or PMS. I'm almost forty years old and I'm more confused than ever. There's only a few things you can do when you see a woman coming toward you who says she's having 'one of those days'—get ready to duck, run, or hand her a fistful of Kleenex."

Since that incident, Scott's actually learned a better coping strategy. When he realizes my hormones are acting up, he brews me a nice cup of tea, leads me to the bedroom, covers me up with a cozy quilt, kisses my furrowed brow, then tiptoes out the door, closing it gently behind him—and locks and bolts it for about three days.

Seriously, I get more mail about PMS than any other issue. Women are coming out of their bolted rooms and uniting as Sisters in Hormone-y. They're frantically searching for relief from this syndrome that wreak its monthly havoc on our emotions, not to mention our marriages and our children. Women especially love when I openly share about one of my worst hormone fits ever. For those of you who haven't heard about the Dairy Queen Episode—I offer it here for your astonishment.

During one particularly stress-filled, premenstrual week, I didn't get the help I needed bringing the groceries in from the car. So, of course, after hauling a gallon jug of milk from the car, I threw it against the wall of the entry hall. Boy, did I regret THAT little burst of temper. A few weeks later, I was again bringing in the groceries and I asked the boys to get up and help me unload the car. My second born, Zeke, started to complain, but just in time, Zach—older and wiser—intervened.

"Hey, Zeke, better jump up and salute. Mom's standing near dairy products."

Laughing about PMS helps us cope with it. And believe me, if my mail is any indication of the general female population, we women will take any coping method we can get! Our poor husbands are just as bumfuzzled as we are. (I'd like to write a book on this subject and call it *PMS Sufferers and the Men Who Are Terrified of Them.*) Actually, there are several things you can do to help.

Here's a practical list that may serve as a good resource for those of you fighting the monthly Pre-Monster Syndrome:

- Think EASY: Expect less of yourself, clear your calendar, read light fluff.

- If you're looking for medical help, I'd recommend seeing a good endocrinologist first, one that specializes in hormones. Many women are helped by taking a natural progesterone.

- My doctor, a woman and a wonderful believer, says, "Becky, if only women would just come in to see me and talk about this! Christian women are the worst about keeping this bottled up inside. They're so ashamed of the way their behavior changes, believing it's a spiritual failure. It's a chemical, hormonal problem, and I have so many things I can do now to help. I've got whole families thanking me for helping Mom!"

- Read *Emotional Phases of a Woman's Life*, by Jean Lush. My husband found tremendous relief when he read the portion of this book describing the typical mood changes in a woman's cycle—he saw I wasn't crazy. Well, maybe I was crazy, but so were 70% of the female population for about one week a month. Focus on the Family has several interviews with this delightful English lady and Dr. Dobson. You can order them by calling 1-800-A-FAMILY and asking for any interviews with Jean Lush.

- Call a hotline for help: PMS Access at 1-800-222-4PMS. This service offers a wide variety of helps and information on women's health issues.

- I'm a real believer in health food supplements. (I still eat junk food, but I like those easy-to-take supplements!) If you have a health food store nearby, ask the owner for advice on some herbs and vitamins for PMS. Read up on the current research, and ask your doctor if there's anything in the product that could hurt you. The American Medical Association is starting to recognize the health benefits of many herbs, oils, and vitamin products.

- Exercise. I hate this word, but I know that a long bike ride or walk is a wonderful way to work out frustrations and trim thighs at the same time. I'm going to do it, too. Tomorrow.

- Curl up with a mug of something warm and soothing, wrap yourself in a quilt, turn on some peaceful praise music, and pray for God's loving arms to surround you, for assurance of His love no matter how you're feeling.

Here's to my suffering Sisters in Hormone-y Land! Why don't we all stop for a moment, take a swig of milk (straight out of the jug shall we?), then say, "Ahhh..." as we wipe the mustache from our upper lip with the back of our hand in triumph. Why? For having the amazing self-control not to throw the container against the nearest wall.

We women need to claim small victories wherever we can find them.

◆ ◆ ◆

I have told you these things, so that in me you may have peace. In this world you will have trouble. But take heart! I have overcome the world.

JOHN 16:33

A man'll seem like a person to a woman....Then one day he'll do something maybe no worse than what he's been a-doing all his life. She'll look at him. And without no warning he'll look like a varmint.

—Marjorie Kinnan Rawlings

T-shirts for Women with PMS

Next mood swing: 6 minutes.

Warning: I have an attitude and I know how to use it.

Do NOT start with me. You will NOT win.

5 Signs You Have PMS

• Everyone around you has an attitude problem.

• You're adding chocolate chips to your cheese omelet.

• The dryer shrunk every last pair of your jeans.

• Your husband is suddenly, and enthusiastically, agreeing with everything you say.

• You're gleefully using your cellular phone to dial up every bumper sticker that says, "How's my driving? Call 1-800-***-****."

17

Today? The Truth? Marriage Stinks!

It was bound to happen sometime. It's time to write a chapter extolling the virtues of married life, and right now Scott and I are on the third day of a stand-off. We're not having one of those door-slamming, loud-yelling fights. It's been more of a nagging, simmering deal. If you've been married long, I'm sure you understand. As Amy Levy so aptly put it, "A lover may be a shadowy creature, but husbands are made of flesh and blood."

When I woke up this morning, I thought, *What shall I write today about the institution of marriage?* The bad-little-kid side of me answered, *How about, "It stinks"?* I have to admit, on days like this, marriage is about as tasty as a mouthful of brewer's yeast. Yeah, yeah, yeah, I know marriage is good for me. Yes, it's a miraculous gift from God. I wrote a whole *book* about the importance of a good marriage. But some days authors of marriage books—and marriage counselors, pastors, and I'll bet *even Gary Smalley*—

think that marriage stinks. We know better, but our feelings don't always line up with our heads.

Recently, Scott and I had dinner with an old friend who had come to town on business. He and his wife have had their share of "Marriage 9-1-1" experiences. As we laughed and commiserated on the ups and downs of "hangin' in there with matrimony," our friend said, "During our newly-wed year, someone told me the most encouraging thing."

"Really? What?" I asked, preparing to take notes on the profound answer.

"Well," our friend continued, "I'd been thinking something was terribly wrong with us. I mean, we'd both been raised in terrific Christian homes, read all the Christian books, went to pre-marital counseling, and so—we were all set to experience a perfectly happy Christian marriage. And then, we didn't."

"So what was the 'encouraging thing'?" Scott probed.

"I'm getting to that part. One evening, I ran into this couple I really admired at church. They'd been married a whole year longer than we had and I knew how committed they were to each other. So I asked them, 'How's marriage?' I'll never forget their looking at each other, smiling, then looking back at me and saying, 'Right now, it's the pits.'"

"And this comforted you?"

"Yes! Because I knew we weren't alone! It was in accepting that marriage isn't always fun—*for anybody*—that I found the comfort and courage to keep working at it."

Some of you might assume that because I write and speak highly of marriage our relationship is great. Mostly, it is. But sometimes, it's the pits. We're all in this journey together, guys.

But I can't leave on the note that marriage sometimes stinks. It's not a bad starting place (at least it's honest!), but none of us wants to stay there. As I was rummaging through my desk, I ran across several perceptive quotes from *Light His Fire* by Ellen Kriedman. I needed these reminders. They caused me to pause and evaluate where my focus has been of late. Perhaps they will help you, too.

> "Change seldom, if ever, occurs as a response to a demand."

> "Life is full of problems. So is marriage. It's supposed to be that way. What we don't understand is that conflict faced and resolved equals growth."

> "A man falls in love with a woman because of how she makes him feel *about himself* when he's with her."

> "A good woman inspires a man, a brilliant one interests him, a beautiful woman fascinates him, but it is the sympathetic woman who gets him."

> "Accept who your husband is, don't see him as a bag of potential. You want to see him grow, yes—but don't expect a totally different personality to pop out of this man you fell in love with. Remember, he wants you to 'Make over me, not make me over.'"

> "The human brain is often filled with unconscious negative thoughts. If we *consciously* put in positive thoughts, they'll eventually turn into *unconscious* positive thoughts. Your emotions don't know the difference between real and imaginary, so act *as if* your mate is wonderful. You'll feel better about him and will be surprised to find him growing to fit the image created."

Could this be, in part, why Paul encourages us to think about whatever is true, noble, right, pure, lovely, admirable, excellent, and praiseworthy? (In everything, including our spouses?)

◆ ◆ ◆

Whatever is true, whatever is noble, whatever is right, whatever is pure, whatever is lovely, whatever is admirable—if anything is excellent or praiseworthy—think about such things.... And the God of peace will be with you.

PHILIPPIANS 4: 8,9

I suspect that in every good marriage there are times when love seems to be over.

—Madeleine L'Engle

18

The Ham Sandwich
of Grace

Scott, in his matter-of-fact style, once said something profound. (He's said something profound more than once; it's just that this one quote stands out.) He said, "Most Christians I know who think they're being persecuted for their faith aren't being persecuted for their faith. They're being persecuted for being obnoxious."

Are some of us trying so hard to be right, we're forgetting to be kind? It's like the young child who prayed, "O God, make all the bad people good, and make all the good people nice." How often are Christians losing the "fight for the right" because we lack a spirit of love in *how* we communicate our views to the world? I see this not only in politics and the church at large, but, I'm ashamed to admit, I often see this attitude creeping into my own life. Unfortunately, this is what keeps people from forgiving one another and having a *relaxed joy* in each other's company.

For he who is most gracious wins.

When I allow this truth to sink into my heart, my neck muscles relax, my fists unclench, and I realize that being right isn't more important than showing love.

My beloved Sunday school teacher, Ed Wichern, never ceased to amaze me. With twinkling blue eyes, white beard and effervescent smile, his kind and gentle ways endeared him to everyone. His students learned incredible lessons in human relations watching Ed diffuse potential verbal explosions. He'd nod in the dissenter's direction, affirming him or her as a person worthy of love, and say something like, "Isn't God good—the way He loves every one of us in spite of our differences?" Then he'd deftly turn in his Bible—with those dear, arthritic hands of his—and move us back into the Word of God.

This reminds me of a skillful parent replacing a china cup with a plastic toy—the exchange occurring so swiftly and smoothly the toddler forgoes his tantrum. Ed has expertly diverted a number of adult Sunday school fits.

He who is most gracious wins.

Without love, even the soundest arguments are nothing but hollow words thrown at another who may go away challenged, but untouched and unchanged. Again, I know from hard experience. I've been there—in my own marriage.

A few years back, Scott and I faced an impasse. I'd read all the books and thought I knew all the intellectual answers to our problems (if only Scott would listen!). We both saw a marriage counselor, which helped, but we were still stuck in a state of perpetual defensiveness. Our debate was at a standstill, both of us fighting for our rights, intensely lonely in the battle. The wall between us finally came crumbling down, not because one of us won the great debate. It happened because of—well, a ham sandwich.

We were on vacation, and I was reading a book on the beach—probably a book on how to have a successful marriage. Suddenly I felt a shadow looming over me. Shading my eyes, I peered upward. There stood Scott, smiling and holding out a plain ham sandwich, like a little boy offering a weed to his mother.

White bread, ham, and a few sprinkles of sand.

But just as a weed seems like a prized orchid when it's offered from the hand of a child, the sandwich looked gourmet to me. For I was starving—not just for food, but for the emotional nourishment of feeling cared for by my mate. I swallowed a lump in my throat, thanked my husband for his thoughtfulness and there we sat together in silence, sharing the meager picnic lunch, sipping Dr. Peppers, and watching blue-green waves lap at the shore.

Later that afternoon, we went back to our room, put down our boxing gloves, left our respective debate platforms, and melted into each other's arms. Months of coldness vanished with the presentation of one sand-sprinkled ham sandwich. That night I wrote the following entry in my notebook.

Ham Sandwich

It was only a simple ham sandwich
But I was hungry—and my husband fed me
I was thirsty—he gave me drink
and deep inside a dam burst and exploded
A simple kindness
To me
For no reason
Why am I so overwhelmed with this gift?

Scott, too, had argued his side of our problems for a long time. But I couldn't hear him until I was emotionally fed, secure of his care and concern for me. For love, expressed in kindness, permits us to unfold.

Yes, he who is most gracious wins.

◆ ◆ ◆

Words from a wise man's mouth are gracious.

ECCLESIASTES 10:12

One advantage of marriage, it seems to me, is that when you fall out of love with him, or he falls out of love with you, it keeps you together until maybe you fall in again.

—Judith Viorst

The Value of a Hug

When a husband shows his wife affection, he sends the following messages:

- I'll take care of you and protect you. You are important to me and I don't want anything to happen to you.

- I'm concerned about the problems you face, and I'm with you.

- I think you've done a good job, and I'm so proud of you.

- A hug can say any and all of the above. Men need to understand how strongly women need these affirmations. For the typical wife, there can hardly be enough of them.[1]

—Dr. Willard F. Harley, Jr.

19

The Power of "I Give Up"

I was lying on my bed face up, tears flowing into my ears. (I cried a lot in my mid-thirties. From what I read and hear from my friends, it's a fairly common occurrence.) I'd just had an argument with Scott, and my marriage seemed to be stuck in an unending pattern: Get along two weeks, fight one week, get along two, fight one more. I was as desperately tired of this pattern as I'd been of my own struggle to be the perfect woman.

I wanted to relax and hold hands with our marriage. I wanted us to lean into one another the way some old couples do who know they're truly One in the most mysterious of ways—not just two people walking the same path because it's the right thing to do.

"Okay, God," I wailed internally. *"You know I've read 106 books on how to make a marriage grow up and fly right. We've gone to counseling. We've filled out personality graphs. I've even tried the 'seduce him in Saran wrap' trick. What else do You want me to DO?"*

At that moment, I reached over and picked up a book from the nightstand. *The Confident Woman* by Anabel Gillham. *Hmmm.*...As I randomly flipped the pages, I stopped at a chapter where Anabel described a technique she uses to "let go of burdens." It involved releasing a helium balloon to the sky, as a symbol of giving a problem to God, then recording the released burden on a piece of paper and keeping it in a dated envelope.

As I scanned the page, my eyes fell on Anabel's words: "In complete desperation...I gave my son to the Lord." The next line caused me to swallow hard—"I have an envelope to prove that I did. It has 'June 27, 1976 A.M. God' written on the outside."

June 27, 1976. June 27, 1976! On the very same day and year that Anabel gave her son's medical condition to the Lord, Scott and I stood trembling before an altar, two teenagers with more hormones than brains, repeating vows that would bind us together forever—and prove nearly impossible to live up to.

I was stunned. Sure, I'd just asked God for guidance, but it had been more like a rhetorical prayer. I certainly didn't expect Him to answer me so clearly—and quickly. But as I read about letting go, and stared at our wedding date written on the page in front of me, I couldn't deny this was a God thing. He may as well have picked up a megaphone, put it to my ear, and shouted: "Here's a little hint for you, Becky: Let Go. Give Up. Helium your efforts and let Me have your marriage." So I did.

Not long after that day, Scott took me out to dinner. As we sipped coffee, he paused and looked me full in the face.

"Becky," he began, "I just want to tell you that I am so sorry for the pain I've caused in our marriage. I want to become better friends, closer lovers..." His words were an unsolicited gift of grace, allowing me to open my heart and confess my own failures as a wife. I'd done nothing to manipulate Scott into this reconciliation. I'd simply let go of the struggle. It would be the first of many times I'd discover that God does amazingly well without my help.

Catherine Marshall often spoke about the power of the Prayer of Relinquishment. This is the prayer we finally utter after we've researched and finagled, after we've knocked ourselves out going to seminars and listening to self-improvement tapes. It's the prayer we sob while lying on our backs, tears dripping into our ears. It's the prayer of "I give up, Lord. I can't do this on my own." And this is the point where God enters.

◆ ◆ ◆

...God has come to help his people.

LUKE 7:16

Love is surrender.

—Ralph Carmichael

When We Give Up, God Comes In

He is always coming. Coming to serve us, when we need it… And coming to save us, when we need that, the way He saved Peter from drowning (Matthew 14:22-33), or the woman caught in adultery, who in another way was also drowning (John 8:1-11). He comes to save us from ourselves mostly, but from the world, the flesh, and the Devil, too. And since we're always in some way in need of saving, He is always in some way coming."[1]

20

In Praise of "The Silent Treatment"

The radio interviewer says, "We've been discussing the sometimes hilarious, sometimes painful subject of marriage, and now, here's your chance to dial 'Marriage 9-1-1'!"

I say a silent prayer for wisdom. The first caller is an ex-Marine, struggling to keep his voice from breaking. "Becky," he says, "I'm losing my wife and I don't know what to do. She's going out every night. I think she's seeing someone else. I've begged her to stay—on my knees even—but nothing I do works." It's a tragic variation of a common heartache. Another scenario is the Christian woman who determined she'd be the Total Woman to an emotionally abusive or negligent husband—and eventually wound up feeling more like the *Totaled* Woman, exhausted from her failed efforts. What to do? Each of these, I believe, is known in professional counseling circles as "a toughie." In cases like this, The Silent Treatment may be in order.

Now before I get mail informing me that The Silent Treatment is a dysfunctional passive-aggressive method of dealing with conflict, consider, for a moment the following. When Jesus was falsely accused and grossly mistreated by a raging mob, He spoke amazingly little in His own defense. When Herod questioned Jesus "with many words," Jesus answered him "nothing." Quiet, controlled, confident, powerful—His very silence spoke volumes. Pilate observed all this—Jesus' manner, His eyes, the way He held Himself even as He suffered—and Pilate knew without a doubt he was condemning an innocent man.

When we're faced with someone whose anger (or mistreatment of us) is out of control, beyond the realm of logic, silence is often the most powerful response. Drawing on Jesus' example, Peter encouraged women to win their wayward husbands "without a word" by their quiet and respectful behavior (1 Peter 3:1-3). Obviously wives are to respect their husbands. But "quiet and respectful behavior" encompasses more than this, for Peter isn't asking a woman to project a hangdog, doormat silence here. Peter is talking Power Packed Quietness. This is not a "treat me however you like, for I'm a lowly worm" silence. This is a silence that conveys, "I know I'm precious to God. My life is one of supreme respect: for God, for His creation, for you, and for myself." (1 Peter 2:9, 3:4). If you can harness this calm, quiet assurance, especially in the heat of conflict, you'll find yourself operating out of strength, not weakness.

Some of the best advice I've ever read for people who are experiencing a major crisis in their marriage is in James Dobson's book *Love Must Be Tough*. To a spouse who has been responding to blatant mistreatment with knee-jerk, emotional outbursts, Dr. Dobson writes, "Instead of begging, pleading, wringing your hands, and whimpering like an abused puppy, you as the vulnerable partner must appear strangely calm and assured. The key word is *confidence*, and it is of maximum importance. Your manner should say, 'I believe in me. I'm no longer afraid. I can cope, regardless of the outcome. I know something I'm not talking about. I've had my day of sorrow and I'm through crying. God and I can handle whatever life puts in the path.'" It's interesting how closely this attitude parallels Christ's when He was mistreated and misunderstood.

And how often it is the ONLY hope for turning around a partner who's heading in the wrong direction.

◆ ◆ ◆

In quietness and trust is your strength.

Isaiah 30:15

I have often regretted my speech, but never my silence.

—Anonymous

The Power of Silence

Harmful Silent Treatment

• Your motivation is to hurt, punish, get revenge.

• It's a manipulative tactic used to get your way in every minor argument.

• You're quiet because you feel powerless, depressed, hopeless.

• You use "loud-and-clear" hateful facial expressions to make up for your shortage of words.

Healing Silent Treatment

Your motive is to bring a change in your relationship, a calm to the chaos. You realize that you are, in actuality, respecting your mate by asking him to respect you, too. (Just as we love our kids when we require they treat us with respect.)

You feel a calm assurance and a freedom to enjoy other things in your life. Sure, there's always a little dull ache when our marriage isn't great, but life doesn't have to stop. Do something wonderful you've always wanted to do while you're waiting for communication to flow again in your marriage. Connect with friends—you can tell them briefly that you're hurting and need their prayers, but don't use the time to dissect the misery in your marriage. Use it as a positive outlet to lift your spirits. Have fun! Nourish yourself.

This is the Biggie. Don't enjoy this quiet period of detachment so much that you're not willing to reconnect again. A mature marriage partner walks a delicate tightrope between independence (relying on God as our source of love) and acknowledging our basic human need for connection. Using a helpful silent treatment should be somewhat like unplugging a shorted-out phone line. A temporary disconnection may be necessary, but the ultimate goal is a clearer, better connection over the long haul.

Sometimes, silence is not only golden, it's downright healing.

Part V

◆ ◆ ◆

What Works–What Doesn't

Time-tested, practical tips that really work!

21

It Works!

The e-mail subject blinked, "It works!" I couldn't wait to open the cyber-file and find out what "it" could be. I read the letter, nodding and chuckling to myself as the story unfolded.

Becky!

I tried one of the techniques in your book *Marriage 9-1-1*—and it worked! Thank you so much for writing that book...especially in the vulnerable way in which you wrote it.

Here's what happened: I asked my husband, Dave, "You think I'm a nice person, right?" (I was a little chicken, so I started off a little generically!!! *smile*) He "nodded obediently" just like you said he would...and I received it just as if he had said it and snuggled into a hug!! It was a wonderful, tender moment...the only trouble was that I had been sanding in our remodeling-in-process-kitchen and the sawdust in my hair tickled his nose so the hug was brief!!!

Becky...thank you, thank you, thank you!! I have such hope for our marriage!

I'll keep you posted!

Love,
Cathie

I turned off the computer and with a satisfied sigh leaned back in my chair. How well I remember the day I came up with this communication technique, one I dubbed the "Help Your Man Meet Your Needs Technique." This is how it works.

Whenever I find myself in need of a hug or words of affection, I find Scott and put my arms around his neck. Then I say, "You think I'm so sweet and pretty you can hardly keep your eyes off me, can you?" He can't resist a smile and obediently nods. I'm fulfilled and happy. Actually, he reports that my putting words in his mouth causes him to realize he really does feel the words. So I'm currently working on this line: "Scott, you just love nicely rounded women. You'd hate to see me lose an ounce, wouldn't you Sweetheart?"

Another practical technique I've found especially helpful is "The Do-Over." You may recall the mid-life crisis cowboy movie, *City Slickers*. In one scene, Billy Crystal's character is trying to console his friend whose marriage has failed and whose life is generally moseying down the sad, lonesome, pitiful trail. Billy tells his friend to remember when they were kids, how they used to have "do-overs"—times when they got to erase the last bad score in a ball game, and try again.

For a real live marriage to survive long-term, you'll have to allow for many starting-over-agains, many "do-overs." You can have big do-overs or small do-overs. You can go fancy and formal and renew your wedding vows in public, or at a candlelight dinner at home in private.

Or you can simply yell, "Cut!" like a director in the middle of a scene and say, "Re-take!" during an everyday, ordinary bad patch of married life. Scott and I often use this technique when we're stuck in a pattern of seemingly endless negativity. (My mother once told me she thinks the default mode of the human brain is negative. We have to consciously put in the positive adjustment.)

What Scott and I do is agree to stop all criticism, pickiness, and destructive comments and only say positive words to each other for an agreed-upon period of time. Say, two weeks. If we're very angry and hurt when we make this agreement, things are remarkably quiet around our house for a couple of days as we rack our brains trying to think of something nice to say to each other.

It's like starting a cold engine. The first words out are mere sputters.

"You look fairly nice today."

"I appreciate that you aren't slurping your cereal this morning."

Then we work up to warmer comments.

"Great tie."

"Good dinner."

But before we know it, we're on a roll of positivity.

"What fun things did you do today?"

"I'm crazy about you, did you know that?"

"I love the way you fixed the dishwasher rack."

"You are a good mother."

"I love you."

The next thing you know, we've moved from "I Can't Believe I Married This Jerk" territory to the "Happily Married—Again" Camp.

Isn't it odd how the simplest things, like a rudder, can turn around a huge ship heading toward a glacier? So it is with a few small changes in the way we react to the one we married. If you're hit a bad patch on the marital road, try these techniques. You might just discover, as Cathie did, "Hey! It works!"

◆ ◆ ◆

Well done....Because you have been trustworthy in a very small matter, take charge of ten cities.

LUKE 19:17

The scripture emphasizes that much can come from little if the little is truly consecrated to God.

—Francis Schaeffer

22

Speaking My Language

So you're familiar with the five love languages?" asked Brenda as we breakfasted, this time at IHOP, over two Rooty Tooties, Fresh and Fruity.

The topic was marriage. Again. How to make it survive and thrive. I'd just confessed that after researching and writing for three years, I felt I was familiar with every marriage improvement technique known to couplehood. However, I now had to admit that somehow I'd missed the Love Language Exchange Program.

Brenda was quick to pull me up to speed. "Okay, here's the brief version of Dr. Gary Chapman's theory. We all have love banks inside us that are filled in different ways. Let's say one person feels most loved when they are given lots of compliments. Their love language is 'verbal affirmation.' Another language is physical touch. These are the folks who need lots of hugs and backrubs and..."

"Let me guess—sex."

"Well, yes. With guys especially. Women typically long for more non-sexual hugs and touches."

"Is there a language of chocolate?" I asked.

"In a way," Brenda replied, smiling. "There's 'receiving gifts.' So, I guess if Scott gave you a box of chocolates…"

"He'd be speaking my language."

"You got it. The last two languages are 'quality time' and 'acts of service.'"

On the way home, I stopped off at a bookstore, picked up a copy of *The Five Love Languages* and studied it with interest. Though I do have a great affinity for chocolate, I quickly surmised that my prime love language was not "receiving gifts," but "verbal affirmation." Mark Twain once said he could survive two months on one good compliment. Without verbal affirmation, my love bank goes bankrupt in about 24 hours. If I were a homeless person walking the streets, I'm convinced my hand-scribbled sign would read, "Will Work for Affirmation," or "Will Fish for Compliment."

That evening, I showed the book to Scott and tried to determine his love language. "Compliments don't seem to ch-ching your bank," I said. "And you've never really acted excited over a gift."

Scott pointed to the table of contents. "I think my heart hears the stuff on the last half of that list—physical touch, quality time, and acts of service."

"Hey, you can't have THREE of them!" I protested. "I only picked 'verbal affirmation.'"

"Yeah, but your bank takes constant deposits. I can go longer between fill-ups."

The next morning, before opening my eyes, I heard Scott's voice, low and gentle: "Good morning, oh beautiful and ravishing wife."

Sleepily, I replied, "I love it when you call me ravishing."

"Listen, Becky," Scott continued, "Could you possibly take my shirts to the dry cleaners this morning on your way to the airport?"

I sat up, wiping the sleep from my eyes and grinned. "So basically, you're trying to exchange one verbal affirmation for one act of service, right?"

"Well," he replied, "it might be nice."

"Alrighty then," I said, feeling strangely as though I were playing a hand of poker. "I'll give you one trip to the dry cleaners for one 'you're ravishing' and one cup of coffee in bed. Don't forget the cream."

"You drive a hard bargain," he mumbled as he walked toward the kitchen and the coffee maker.

By mid-afternoon, I was heading to the airport for a speaking engagement when, with embarrassed remorse, I realized I'd forgotten to take Scott's shirts to the cleaners.

I grabbed my car phone and dialed him at work. "Scott," I apologized, "I just blew my 'act of service.' I'm so sorry, but I forgot to drop off the shirts and now I'm…"

"Leaving on a jet plane? Don't know when you'll be back again?" Scott deadpanned.

"Oh, Babe I hate to go," I sang back with Peter, Paul, and Mary angst. "You can take back the 'ravishing' compliment if you want to."

"It's okay, Becky. No big deal."

"You're being so nice about this."

I could almost see Scott's mischievous grin through the telephone as he said, "I'm just saving up love bank points. Have a good time, Mrs. Ravishing."

We said good-bye, then I glanced at the backseat and the shirts untaken and the simple forgiveness offered in spite of my forgetfulness. "I do not at all understand the mystery of grace," writes Anne Lamott, "only that it meets us where we are but does not leave us where it found us."

I realized with a rush of gratitude that I'd just been given a small deposit by one wonderful husband. My account overflowed, and the love language, freely spoken, was grace.

◆ ◆ ◆

Freely you have received, freely give.

MATTHEW 10:8

Marriage involves big compromises all the time. International-level compromises. You're the USA, he's the USSR, and you're talking nuclear warheads.

—Bette Midler

23

The Way to a Man's Heart
Is Through Your Ears

I t was a rare and precious evening. Scott and I were curled up on an overstuffed loveseat, our legs outstretched and intertwined together on the giant ottoman in front of us. He was drinking a mug of hot black coffee, I was sipping herbal tea from a china cup. In the background, romantic music from the 1940s played. *Sentimental Journey. You Made Me Love You.* The room was softly illuminated by the light of a lamp and a glowing fire in the hearth.

After traveling all day and speaking to a gathering of bankers' wives, my feelings that night were a mixture of gratitude, relief, exhaustion, and satisfaction. Ruby Kathryn, the benevolent woman who organized the day's event had seen to it that our time in Mississippi included plenty of Southern-style pampering. Knowing Scott was accompanying me, she'd arranged for our stay in that charming bed-and-breakfast. She'd even sent a dozen red roses and a gargantuan basket of goodies to our room. I felt like saluting the South, its charm, and all its Ruby Kathryns.

Not only was that evening special because of the romantic setting away from home, kids, and phone; it was unusual because I wasn't in the mood for talking. I'd talked nonstop all afternoon and for the moment, anyway, had grown weary of the sound of my own voice. I was in a curious frame of mind—I was in the mood for *listening*. For a few moments there was silence between us, except for Nat King Cole's crooning, the crackle of burning logs, and an occasional sigh of contentment.

Then something remarkable happened. I asked my husband a couple of questions. Then I focused on his face, listening attentively to his answers. Allowing Scott all the time he needed, I didn't interrupt or interject my own thoughts, as is so often my habit. Oh, occasionally I threw in a piggyback question or encouraging comment, but mostly I gently batted the conversational ball back into his court. Amazing. Like a bud opening to flower, I sat in that cozy atmosphere and observed my husband come to life.

My reserved husband smiled as he chatted away the hour. One might even say he was *animated* as he poured out several dreams, plans, and ideas he'd been mulling over for months. He was relating on a deeper level than he had in a long, long time. I realized how happy he seemed at that moment, how starved he'd probably been for the listening ear of a wife who, of late, had been far too preoccupied with herself.

I also realized another truth: Men don't stop talking because they aren't talkers by nature. They stop talking because we stop *really listening*. They stop talking because when they do talk, we criticize them, or tease about their subject choice, or judge them, or interrupt them with our views. How long had it been since I'd simply listened, with sincere attentiveness, to Scott? How long had it been since I'd let go of my own agenda and been there for *him*— encouraging and complimenting his terrific thoughts and ideas?

◆ ◆ ◆

Back home in Texas, mulling over that night of intimate communication, I thought of all the books I've read (and written!) filled with ways to encourage your husband—all of them good and helpful. Be playful. Be romantic. Tell him how much you admire him. But perhaps the most effective method of encouraging your husband—*simply listening*—is usually brushed over or completely ignored.

Dr. Robert Fisher has written a powerful little book called *Quick To Listen, Slow To Speak*. In it he describes being on a long car ride with a man he'd never met before. Fisher writes, "To my surprise, as I paid close attention to what he was saying, I found myself genuinely interested and involved in the conversation. Occasionally I would make a comment or ask a pertinent question, but I was never asked and never gave any information about myself." At the end of the long ride, the companion said to Dr. Fisher, "I know you're young, but I want you to know you are absolutely one of the finest conversationalists I have ever met."

I ponder the simple power of listening as I read that story. I can count on one hand, maybe two, the people in my life who've gifted me with complete and focused attention— who acted as if they had nothing more exciting to do than listen to me, to try to understand the way I think and feel about life or donuts or whatever. They leave me feeling so— *affirmed*. My mother does this beautifully. My husband, bless his heart, listens more than his fair share in our relationship. And I have a sprinkling of friends I hold especially dear because they make me feel supremely loved by simply listening to me attentively and with compassion. I wholeheartedly agree with Dr. Fisher when he writes, "Rapt and exclusive attention is one of the greatest gifts we can give another individual. It is the highest form of compliment."

For centuries men have found themselves, in a weaker moment, wrapped in the arms of a mistress—and not because of the woman's superior beauty or sexual expertise, as is often assumed. Men have always been most susceptible to women who listen to them with interest, admiration, acceptance, and respect. The apostle Paul writes, "And let the wife see that she respects and reverences her husband—that she notices him, regards him, honors him, prefers him, venerates, and esteems him; and that she defers to him, praises him and loves and admires him exceedingly" (AMP). Why? For many reasons, but one important one is if we don't listen to, notice, and esteem our husbands, we leave them vulnerable to women who will gladly take over for us.

Scott's an extremely handsome man. He's also sensitive and kind-hearted—a big-time attractive quality to women. Not only that, but he's also employed in a non-profit organization as the only male among fifty-two female coworkers. "Wow," women comment, "that has to be scary for you." Well, it could be. And at times, when our relationship was shakier, it was. But I don't worry about it much anymore. Sure, a beautiful young woman may attract his eye, but I know it's the woman who loves Scott enough to listen to his dreams and deepest fears that will keep his heart. And I aim to stay that woman.

"When someone deeply listens to you," writes poet John Fox, "it is like holding out a dented cup you've had since childhood and watching it fill up with cold, fresh water. When it balances on top of the brim, you are understood. When it overflows and touches your skin, you are loved." It's a challenge for us women of the "verbal variety," to listen fully, deeply, and actively to our husbands. But oh, the rewards of watching their cup overflow with love.

◆ ◆ ◆

My dear brothers, take note of this: Everyone should be quick to listen, slow to speak.

JAMES 1:19

I wished a companion to lie near me in the starlight, silent and not moving, but ever within touch.

—Robert Louis Stevenson

Top Ten Ways to Lend an Ear of Encouragement

1. *Listen intentionally*—it is a conscious act of the will (especially for those of us who are out of practice).

2. *Plan ahead* for times and places, free of interruptions, that are conducive to unhurried conversation. (I'd highly recommend the B&B in Tupelo, Mississippi.)

3. Use good *eye contact*—don't let yourself get easily distracted. (Don't you just hate it when you're pouring out your heart to someone and out of the blue they avert their eyes from you to focus on something more interesting—like, say, a fruit fly?)

4. *Ask questions that are pertinent* to what has just been said; don't suddenly shift topics. (Switching gears like this is on par with telling your spouse, "You know all the stuff you've just shared? It's boring me to tears, so could we change the subject? Like *now*?")

5. *Listen understandingly*, with an open heart rather than defensively. (Translation: No plotting how we can defend our

viewpoint as soon as our spouse takes a breath.)

6. *Perceive the context*—is your husband tired, in pain, angry, frustrated? Occasionally, we all lash out in an emotional outburst and say things we don't mean. When Scott is angry or fatigued, I've found it helpful to look at him in much the same way I would view a toddler in need of a nap. I don't absorb anything he says too seriously until he's calmed down or had some rest. Sometimes the best thing a wife can do for her husband is simply allow him to "vent." (Within reason, of course. We all have our limits!)

7. *Listen Actively*—be willing to act on what your husband is asking of you if at all possible. In other words, don't let it go "in one ear and out the other."

8. *Don't interrupt*—This is tough, but remember Proverbs 18:13 says, "He who answers before listening—that is his folly and his shame."

9. *Be patient*—men tend to save the best for last. Encourage them when they share about everyday occurrences (yes, even a sports game), and eventually, they'll move

on to a deeper level of sharing—all that "touchy-feeling" stuff most of us women love to hear.

10. *Practice "by the way" conversation—* with men who are shy about talking, it helps to first join them in any kind of activity they enjoy. (Yes, I did say *any* kind of activity they enjoy.) As you relax and have fun together, their talking tends to happen naturally, "by the way."

24

Little Miracles

The Ten-Second Miracle. Wow, what a great title, I thought, as I picked up the book and scanned its contents. In this instant age, we want cures—and fast. Who couldn't use a zippy miracle or two?

Within ten seconds, my decision was made. I bought the book.

Moments later, I was wedging myself into an airplane seat, readying for the flight home to Texas. Once settled, I opened to the first chapter.

In the first paragraph, the author and psychiatrist, Gay Hendricks, wrote "You are never more than ten seconds away from a breakthrough in the most important area of your life. I base this news on a careful study of more than three thousand sessions in which real people healed real relationship problems."

Within ten seconds of reading, I was intrigued enough to continue.

As I read though the entire volume, I encountered some areas I didn't agree with, but I became fully convinced of the truth of the central premise: our relationships move closer or stagnate in micro-time increments. Also, the most important things are often said in one-breath sentences: one heartfelt, inarguable, vulnerable statement.

It's been said that the most important and precious words conveyed at family reunions occur in the last few seconds— before we say our good-byes. "You're doing so well with your life." "You know I'm here for you if you need anything at all." "I'm proud of you." "I love you!" "Your kids are wonderful, what great parents you are." "Lean on the Lord, Sweetheart, He's always been there for me."

It's little things that bring relationships closer. It also takes so little to tear them apart. One poetic soul wrote, "It's not love's going that haunts my days, but that it went in little ways."

As I pondered these thoughts, I began jotting down some typical everyday "miracle" phrases we might hear in marriages that are drawing closer, second by second, year upon year.

> "Your skill amazes me."

> "I'm feeling a little scared these days. Can you hold me a minute?"

> "You're a great dad to our kids, did you know that? I don't know how I'd raise them without you."

> "I love those little lines—those little half-parenthesis —that show up on the sides of your face when you smile. Lights up my whole day to see you this happy."

"I'm sorry I'm so cranky today. It has nothing to do with you, I'm just tired. You want to curl up and spoon together for a nap?"

"I blew it. My bad. Forgive me?"

"Remember how we used to kiss when we were dating? Want to try it again?"

"I've been thinking about you all day. I just had to hear your voice."

"It's been awhile since we've had a date. Will you go out with me?"

"Come here—the radio's playing my favorite love song and I want to dance with you."

"You're pregnant! WOW! This is great! WOW!"

"This is delicious. Better than my mom's..."

"Take the day off and relax. I'll watch the baby, you go shopping and have a ball with the girls."

"You just put your feet up and watch the game—I'll make some nachos and we'll eat in the living room."

"What? You think I'm attracted to HER? She doesn't hold a candle to you, Babe. No one could."

"Bless your heart...rough day?"

"They just don't know how wonderful you are, that's all."

"Can I get you something while I'm up?"

"What can I do to help get ready for company?"

"You are NOT fat. You are curvaceous. Like Marilyn Monroe."

"Would you like to join me for a cup of coffee on the porch swing?"

"Your neck looks uncomfortable all bent up like that on the couch arm. Can I get you a pillow?"

"I'll never leave you. I can't imagine my life without you."

"I have to stay up late and finish this project, but could I get my goodnight kiss before you head off to bed?"

"I'll clean up the kitchen. You take a long bath. Then let's meet in the bedroom in twenty minutes."

"Happy Anniversary, Darling. We've made it thirty years! The thirty best years of my life..."

"I'll always love you."

"Wrinkles look great on you. And that gray hair—it makes you look so handsome and distinguished. So Cary Grant."

"Even if the news is bad, I'll be there for you. You won't have to face anything alone. Ever."

"I need you to pray for me."

"It's been an amazing fifty years. You're still my Sweetheart, you know that?"

"Don't cry, Darling. I'll be all right."

"I don't want to say good-bye to you, it's the hardest thing I've ever done."

"I'll be waiting for you inside heaven's gate, my Love."

I'll leave you, my friends, with my own twist on the earlier "little ways" quote.

"It is love growing that graces my days, and that it comes in little ways."

Would that this would be true for all of you, one ten-second miracle at a time.

◆ ◆ ◆

The right word at the right time is like a custom-made piece of jewelry.

PROVERBS 25:11 THE MESSAGE

And what do all the great words come to in the end, but that?— I love you—I am at rest with you—I have come home.

—**Dorothy L. Sayers**

25

Wanna Play?

Y ou may have observed that most young children, given a simple stick and a backyard and a big blue sky, can find a thousand ways to have fun. There's doodle bug pushing. Outlining clouds. There's jumping over, on, and around the stick. Not to mention throwing it, twirling it, banging it, and stirring mud with it. What happened to that childlike ability to make fun out of the simplest things? Ever notice how we "mature" couples tend to turn even *fun*—something that used to be so easy and spontaneous—into a planned, programmed, complicated event?

Recently I received a wonderful letter from an old buddy that not only touched my heart and funnybone, but poignantly reminded me of how we often complicate our lives by neglecting childlike fun. Here's an excerpt from the opening.

Dear Becky,

I've learned that to combat the temptations that plague a working man's idle time when he's on a business trip, nothing quite satisfies like a good book, and I don't mean Larry Crabb or Chuck Colson. They're great, but when I'm traveling, I need a book to entertain me. So it must have been Providence that I picked up a copy of *Marriage 911* on my way to the airport. My mom had told me, Becky, that you had written your third book. I said, "You can't mean Becky Arnold! She used to think chicken eggs and grocery store eggs came from different places!"

(Ahhhh, at least some character traits of my youth carried over into my adulthood. Naïveté is still one of my well-known fortes.) Then my friend's letter took on a more sobering note, as he confessed how hard he and his wife had struggled to make their marriage all they knew it could be.

Your book struck me deeply in several ways. First of all, I think your ideas about loving each other and liking each other are right on. (My wife and I) have been to so much counseling over the years that marriage has at times become our mutual thorn in the flesh....You get to working so hard on your counseling assignment that your spouse becomes your project, and a constant reminder of your inadequacy...

So, lesson #1 for me: Don't work so hard that you forget to have fun.

Isn't that a great truth? In *Still Lickin' the Spoon,* I describe a Sunday afternoon when two friends called and asked me spontaneously to "go out to play." "What could I do?" I asked the reader rhetorically. "I had no choice but to tell Scott it was obviously the will of God that I go." My girlfriends and I had an idyllic afternoon at a park on a quilt watching brightly colored hot air balloons take off one after another and eating smoked ears of corn on the cob slathered with butter and sour cream. I recalled wiping some of the drippy deliciousness off my face with the back of my hand, grinning at my friends, and declaring, "Life doesn't get any better than this."

I have to admit that my family ended up eating sandwiches and cleaning up after themselves that afternoon, but what my husband and children did get out of the deal was a wife and mother who came home smiling and refreshed and happy to be alive. They agreed it was a pretty good trade-off.

Watch for the rainbow of opportunities to be a grown-up kid. Sail Styrofoam boats, fly kites, ride a hot-air balloon, eat greasy fair food, blow silly noises through straws. Just do something each day on which you can look back and say, "I did that for the sheer, simple, childlike fun of it."

What would happen to our lives if we stopped more often and seized the moments God gives us full of pure, *unadult*-erated fun? And what would happen to our marriages if, every now and then, we invited our mates to come along for the ride?

◆ ◆ ◆

God…richly provides us with everything for our enjoyment.

1 TIMOTHY 6:17

A good and wholesome thing is a little harmless fun in this world; it toness a body up and keeps him human and prevents him from souring.

—**Mark Twain**

26

Down-Home Tips
for Worn-Out Marriages

Over 900 books have been written about marriage in the last ten years. Now, I'm a nutshell kind of gal—always searching for the bottom line. So I was thinking, *What, in a nutshell, do those 900 books have to say?*

Having read at least 100 of those volumes—and having recently added two of my own books on marriage to the pile—I've discovered the steps to mending a worn-out marriage can basically be summed up in six down-home tips. So if your marriage is in the Danger Zone (or you know someone else's who is), you might want to copy this list and keep it handy as a Marital Emergency Guide.

Down-Home Tip Number One:
Know When to Yelp for Help

In *Marriage 911*, I compared the feelings of hurting couples to those of accident victims. Scott and I were both so wounded at times, neither of us had the strength to help the other. It was time to call a paramedic—in the form of a marriage counselor.

One word of caution: In choosing a counselor, look for one who imparts hope, who helps you believe that you *can* recover and, with time and effort, find love again. When a couple latches onto a hope-filled vision of their Marriage-in-the-Future, half the battle is already won.

Remember, also, to ask Christ—The Wonderful Counselor—to lead you personally to pertinent Scriptures, good books, taped or live marriage seminars, relationships with other couples, or even special songs that may awaken loving feelings.

Down-Home Tip Number Two: Sweep the Junk Off the Porch

Have you ever fantasized about starting over with someone who doesn't have your Background of Faults stored in their personal files? Who hasn't?

But unless we plan to repeatedly start over every time we mess up in a relationship, we all periodically have to sweep the junk off the porch with a broom of forgiveness. Starting over is possible *within the same marriage*. It happens when forgiveness is allowed to do its cleansing work.

Someone also once wisely pointed out that "Forgiveness is like setting a prisoner free, then discovering you were the prisoner all along."

Down-Home Tip Number Three: Focus Your Lens on the Roses, Not the Junk

Picture looking through a camera, focusing on your mate. In his personality, you see some gorgeous roses, but here and there are a couple of junk piles. As the photographer, however, you have the power of focus. Focus on the roses and they'll loom so large and beautiful that quite often the junk disappears altogether from view. So it is with each other. Whatever we focus on enlarges.

What would happen if, instead of obsessing over our mate's problems, we focused and praised each other's strengths?

Down-Home Tip Number Four:
Grow Each Other Up

I believe in the theory that we marry each other, in part, to help us finish childhood. Or as Joseph Barth said, "Marriage is our last best chance to grow up." Inside, aren't we all still a little like toddlers? Especially when we're tired or our affection tanks are low.

Sometimes I'll say to myself, *Scott's over-reacting here— so what's really underneath this?* It's much the same self-questioning we use as parents when our over-tired toddler falls apart over a minor irritation. Do they need punishment or a hug and a nap? Does my mate need a lecture or some loving? Nine times out of ten, it's the latter.

Down-Home Tip Number Five:
Two Parasites Can't Feed on Each Other!

I know this tip sounds gross, but it's a perfect picture of what happens when we expect another person to make us complete.

I was an idealistic 17-year-old bride, certain that Scott would fulfill all my needs. I cried a lot in the early years, always probing him with my insecure questions: "Do you really love me? How much do you love me? Will you always love me?" Then a wise friend told me, "Insecurity didn't attract your husband to you in the first place, Becky, and it won't *keep* him attracted after you're married." As I realized more of God's unconditional love for me, I found a rich, never-changing source of security—and relieved Scott of an impossible burden in the process.

Down-Home Tip Number Six:
Get Out There and Play!

Couples who keep sparking well into their golden years have a sense of humor and playfulness—finding even the idiosyncrasies in each other to be more amusing than maddening.

Like the time I locked my keys in the car. I ran in the house to ask Scott for assistance. He casually strolled out to the car (he's used to these things), reached through the open driver's window, pulled the keys out of the ignition, and, with a smile, handed them to me.

Later that night I heard Scott snickering on his side of the bed.

"What's so funny?" I asked sleepily.

"Oh," Scott replied, "I just keep picturing how cute you looked standing by that open window all worried about your keys."

I laughed, realizing how far we'd come. For the ultimate test of a marriage-on-the-mend is when you find even the stupid things your partner does to have a certain charm about them.

So there you have it—A Marital Emergency Guide in a Six-Point Nutshell. (I know, I know. If only it were as easy to apply them as it is to write them down!)

Does this seem like an awful lot of work to keep two people together in holy matrimony? Well, it is. Especially if you are a high maintenance couple. But I promise you it's worth every effort. In the words of Winston Churchill, "Never, never, never give up."

◆ ◆ ◆

Run in such a way as to get the prize…do not run like a man running aimlessly.

1 CORINTHIANS 9:24

Love doesn't just sit there, like a stone; it has to be made, like bread; re-made all the time, made new.

—Ursula K. Le Guin

Part VI

◆ ◆ ◆

Martha Stewart Doesn't Live Here (In fact, she probably wouldn't want to visit)

Hope for the domestically challenged

27

Hey, Good Lookin', Whatcha Got Burnin'?

For a creative person, it's amazing how badly I've failed in the art of cuisine. My worst handicap in the cooking arena is that I tend to burn everything. One morning, when our son Zeke was about five years old, I handed him a perfectly browned piece of toast. Then I watched in fascination as he grabbed a dinner knife, walked robotically to the trash can, and began scraping at the toast.

"Zeke!" I exclaimed. "Guess WHAT? Mommy didn't burn the toast today—you don't have to scrape it!"

He looked up at me with startled brown eyes and said in surprise, "Oh! I thought we always had to whittle toast." Bless his heart. He thought the normal routine for toast-eating children everywhere was to burn a piece of bread, scrape it, then eat it.

As my children grew older, they began to realize that other families are different in several ways from our own.

Not all families, for example, use the smoke alarm as their dinner bell.

When Zach was a teenager, he strolled into the kitchen one afternoon, where I'd just burnt a cobbler so badly that it had bubbled up, blackened, and hardened into a peculiar sculpture. (Later we all agreed it looked a lot like Ross Perot's ears.) As Zach casually observed the smoke billowing from the oven, heard the smoke alarm blaring, and noted the sweat dripping from my brow—he paused to give me a hug, then cheerfully announced, "Mmmm - mmm - mmm. Smells like Mom's home cooking!"

I used to worry that my kids would go to someone's barbecue and pig out on the charcoal instead of the meat.

Not only do I have a tendency to burn food, but I just can't seem to get the hang of stocking the refrigerator. Scott opened the door to the fridge one day and said, "Becky, I have to hand it to you—you are the Condiment Queen. We have French's mustard, hot mustard, sweet and sour mustard, and relish mustard. And there's no shortage of mayonnaise either—regular, light, Hellman's, Miracle Whip, and no-fat. But there's not a single slice of lunch meat or bread anywhere in the house to put the spreads ON."

"Yes, well..." I started to explain, but Scott was still talking to himself, fiddling with the endless rows of bottles in the door.

"Oh, look!" He held up three red containers for my observation. "Do we ever have ketchup—Heinz, Del Monte, and Sam's Choice! And if it's relish I wanted, I could pick from hot, sweet, sour, chow-chow, and Cajun spice. But lo, I see nary a hot dog or even a lone bun in here. There are 97 bottles of salad dressing, but if there's a shred of lettuce or slice of tomato to make a salad to put under all that dressing, I'm not finding it."

"I can explain..."

"There are little midget pickles, giant pickles, olives—black and green, and seven jars of jelly, jam, and preserves. Becky," he paused for effect, as he turned to face me. "I just want to know one thing. Why do you buy all these condiments?!?"

I shrugged my shoulders. "To make sauces."

"Yes but, Honey," he asked incredulously, "to go on WHAT?"

"I don't know," I stammered. "Pickles and olives?"

Needless to say, Scott and I went out for burgers.

People often ask me how I do all I do. How do I write, speak, enjoy my kids and husband and friends, and also keep up with cooking and cleaning? To tell you the truth, something had to go. I can't do it all. In our home, baking, dusting, and mending are foreign terms to my children. But when you think about it, isn't it good times with our family that we're most hungry for? It's the fun we have as we gather together to ask the Lord's blessing that they'll remember, whether that blessing is over a roast and hot gravy or a take-home sack of spicy tacos.

Besides, my future daughters-in-law will someday have me to thank for the fact that their husbands will never whine, "This homemade apple pie just doesn't taste like my mom's."

Unless, that is, her pies come out of the oven in cinders, to the symphony of smoke alarms.

◆ ◆ ◆

...burnt offerings...you did not desire, nor were you pleased with them.

HEBREWS 10:8

Anybody who believes that the way to a man's heart is through his stomach flunked geography.

—**Robert Byrne**

28

Simplify Your Marriage

Who hasn't noticed the movement to pare down, slow down, and simplify our fast-forward lives? Out of a desire to slow my go-go life to a Mayberry pace, I began writing a book called *A View from the Porch Swing*. One day, as I was sitting on said porch swing, I opened my notebook and jotted some ways my husband and I have simplified our marriage over the years. I offer—Tips for Simple Minded Couples:

1) The Punctual Partner/ Late Mate Dilemma

Nearly every marriage includes one person who lives by a stopwatch, who's struggling to live with a spouse who's running barefoot out the door, shoes in hand, muttering, "Grab my keys—I left them on the counter! I think. Oh, and I also forgot..."

The rub comes when the on-time person believes they can, with effort, TRAIN their mate to be punctual. I have a simple answer for the watch-tapping partner: Forget it. A chronically-late person will always be a chronically-late person. (Isn't that what "chronic" means? On-going, never ceasing?) As you may have guessed, I happen to be the time-impaired party in our union.

If I could start our courtship over, I'd begin by telling Scott, "Look. You should know this up front. I'm a late person. When people introduce me as The Late Becky Arnold, I'm not dead; I'm just running behind. It's what I do—run behind. I see this as a generous way to let others go ahead. I'm friendly, I'm loyal, and I can even be fairly entertaining—once I arrive at my destination, which will be, by the way, at least twenty minutes late. You'll save yourself a lot of grief if you'll just tell me to be ready twenty or thirty minutes earlier than you actually plan to arrive. Think it over carefully. Do you still want to date me? Because the truth is, this is the earliest I've ever been late."

2) The Morning Sunshine/Morning Impaired Conflict

Just as God pairs a late person with a punctual mate, He also pairs morning people with partners who mumble until noon. This is because—well, I don't know. I have no idea why God does this. If anyone out there knows, I would love to hear your theory.

Until we get to heaven, my suggestion to the non-morning marriage partner is—begin training your family early, so one day you may simply avoid functioning in the early morning altogether.

It's taken me years to get to this luxurious stage of life, but I'm no longer an active participant in mornings. Rachel, my responsible daughter, rises early, takes a shower, and wakes up her brothers. Zeke, the closest thing to a gourmet cook in our family (gourmet cook being defined as "one who makes food without charring it"), puts breakfast out. (This took years of training on my part to teach him how to put just the right amount of cold cereal into a bowl and cover it, just so, with milk.) Scott, a morning-kind-of-guy, gets up and enjoys a fatherly chat with the kids, then sends them out the door with a wave. Zeke drives the bunch to school. (A mother's payoff for surviving the Driver's Ed. phase.)

Once the kids are off, Scott often brings me coffee in bed. This, too, took years of training and convincing. One day, my husband realized that a little extra kindness to me in the mornings yields numerous rewards for the rest of the family in the late afternoon and evening. When the kids feel like zombies, I'm cleaning up the kitchen and helping with homework, and there's amorous energy available should I encounter an in-the-mood husband. A win-win solution all around.

In short, one of the best ways to simplify your marriage is to quit trying to *change*—and work *around*—each other's quirks instead.

Guys: Don't pressure your wife to be a Martha Stewart if God designed her to be an Erma Bombeck. (I have a T-shirt that says, "Martha Stewart Doesn't Live Here." I've discovered the nice thing about a laughing home is it doesn't have to be a perfect home.)

Ladies: Many men feel pressured to measure up to some impossible Perfect Christian Man image. It feels about as good to them as it did when women were trying, and failing, to measure up to The Total Woman.

So, cut each other some slack! (Another phrase for "offer grace.") I pray that as you do, you'll find yourself in an authentic Porch Swing marriage, with laid-back joy to spare. What could be more simple?

◆ ◆ ◆

Above all, love each other deeply, because love covers over a multitude of sins.

1 PETER 4:8

Keep your eyes wide open before marriage, half shut afterwards.

—Benjamin Franklin

Too-perfect homemakers beware. Your perfectionism COULD drive you over the deep end someday. I recently received the following warning.

7 Ways to Know if Martha Stewart Is Stalking You

• You get a threatening note made up of letters cut out of a magazine with pinking shears, and they're all the same size, the same font, and precisely lined up in razor-sharp rows.

• You find a lemon slice in the dog's water bowl.

• On her TV show she makes a gingerbread house that looks exactly like your split-level, right down to the fallen licorice downspout and the half-open graham cracker garage door.

• You discover that every napkin in the entire house has been folded into a swan.

• No matter where you eat, your place setting always includes an oyster fork.

• You wake up in the hospital with a concussion and endive stuffing in both ears.

• You awaken one morning with a glue gun pointed squarely at your temple.

29

Aprons and Apple Pies: Nostalgia for "Happy Days"

My mom, Ruthie, is my co-author of *Worms in My Tea* and *Adult Children of Fairly Functional Parents*. Before her retirement, she toyed with the idea of writing a book called *Pearls & Heels—Were the Fifties For Real?* She tells me women didn't really clean house in pearls and high heels—but, yes, the fifties' mindset was real. And in many ways, Mother misses those days and wishes her children and their spouses could have experienced what she calls "this golden blip in time." A nice house and two cars was an affordable dream for most couples of the late '50s and early '60s—and all on one salary. And though the roles men and women were expected to play sometimes stifled growth, Mother tells me there was a certain peacefulness, too, in having a clear-cut division of duty.

Thought I'd take a peek into the '50s to see how this wife of the '90s lines up with June Cleaver. The list below concerned some of the things the average husband expected of his wife—lifted from an issue of *Ladies Home Journal,* circa 1952.

Prepare his breakfast in the morning.

I surprised Scott and brought him coffee in bed one morning. The sight of me awake at that hour, and bearing anything consumable, so startled him—no kidding—he dropped the entire cup upside down on the bedspread.

Serve well-balanced, tasty meals.

Does food of equal weight in both hands—like a Quarter Pounder and a medium Coke—count as "balanced"?

Maintain a tidy, comfortable home.

Let's see…we've been remodeling now for seven years. Scott's building a rock climbing wall on the inside of our stairwell. In the past month, our living room has doubled as a teenager's bedroom and a make-shift kitchen. One day we had to climb over the washer and dryer to get to the refrigerator. So we wouldn't mess up his freshly laid floor tile, my ingenious handyman laid a pattern of two-by-fours for us to balance and walk on to get to the bathroom. (No easy trick with a full bladder.) Needless to say, no one has EVER described our home as tidy. But one teenager wrote me a sweet note saying ours was the most comfortable home she'd ever been in. She loved it because there was nothing she could do to mess it up.

Be a wise and thrifty shopper.

What? You have to be WISE to buy groceries? I'm doing good these days to be conscious and coherent when I'm pushing the cart down what I call the Twilight Zone aisles—

Superstore rows that never come to an end. The year I was teaching school, I used the "Zombie Method" of grocery shopping—falling in behind some perky, organized woman with healthy-looking kids—then dropping everything she put into her cart into mine.

Keep his clothes mended and presentable.

Funny you should ask. My daughter asked me the other day what the word "mend" meant. I told her it was an ancient, archaic word—so old and seldom used these days that "I doubt it's even in the dictionary anymore."

Help entertain his friends and associates.

I must say all of Scott's friends and associates have said at one time or another that I am entertaining—especially when I try to put a company meal together. One of Scott's best friends sat down with us for dinner one evening and finally blurted, "Becky, I've eaten with you guys at least five times now. I never knew weenies could be presented so many different ways—and still taste just as bad every time."

Oh, dear. In my heart of hearts, there's a neatly ironed Laura Petrie just waiting to come out to greet my "Rob" at the door of our neatly kept home, with a hug and kiss and a nice pot roast simmering in the oven.

My own mother came awfully close to this ideal. She never sent my father off to work without a warm kiss and a hot breakfast. While he cat-napped in the lounge chair after "a hard day's work at the office," she put together a real home-cooked meal. Born during the depression, my mother relished her life as a homemaker and never took her freedom from financial and job stress for granted. My admiration for her is high.

Sometimes in especially stressful moments, when my creative right brain mentally ping-pongs from housework to writing deadlines to family needs, and the general "hurry disease" of our decade drags me down, part of me looks back wistfully and wishes the Happy Days of the Fifties were here again.

But then I think of all I DO have and realize, though housework is not my forte, I score high on enjoying my husband and children and friends and my day-to-day routine. Our life isn't simple, but it is rich. Indeed, though I'm more often seen wearing jeans and sporting a bag of bought burgers than donning an apron and presenting a pot roast, I'm realizing these are uniquely *our* Happy Days.

◆ ◆ ◆

Better a bread crust shared in love than a slab of prime rib served in hate.

PROVERBS 15:17 THE MESSAGE

Come, let's be a comfortable couple and take care of each other!

—**Charles Dickens**

Now, HERE'S a lady from the '50s era with whom I can relate.

"Household Hints"

Some 15 years ago, I actually did a household hints column for the local newspaper. To this day, homemakers in the area are still trying to salvage bits and pieces of the damages I caused. Queries on "How do I clean my bathroom?" would get an answer like "Burn incense daily. At the end of five years…move."

What really amazed me was how seriously women took their housekeeping chores…

"How can I prevent scrub water from running down my arm to my elbows?" ("Hang by your feet when you wash the walls?")

"…For mildew or musty odor on the shower curtains, simply take a sharp pair of scissors and whack it off. Actually, the more mildew, the more interesting the shower curtains become…"[1]

—Erma Bombeck

Part VII

◆ ◆ ◆

Forever and Always

Becoming soulmates

30

Not Just Another Pretty Face

A couple of years ago, *Home Life* magazine sent two photographers to take pictures of me for my column. So there I was, all poised, sitting outside on a bench and smiling into the camera, when my husband strolled out the back door. Alan—the *verbal* photographer—looked up and said, "Becky, did you know Scott looks just like one of those *GQ* guys? We really ought to take a few pictures of him."

I like to tell people that at this point Alan walked over, shoved me off the bench and had my husband take my place—because frankly, Scott's a lot prettier than I am. But that's a bit of an exaggeration. I'm just glad I nabbed Scott when I was 15. Don't know if I could hook one this gorgeous again.

I do want you to know that Scott's much more than "just another pretty face." For one thing, he's a man without pretenses. That's why he freely allows me to open the pages of our lives to the public. He's a man's man with a heart of gold. The thought of him brings tender feelings to the surface.

A while back, our little community of Lone Oak was walking around in a daze of pain. One of our "own" (for in little towns, all the kids seem partly ours), a sixteen-year-old boy was thrown from a truck and killed. Zach and Zeke had been at football practice with him just minutes before. Thankfully, Scott was home when our boys came through the front door, grieving and shocked by life's fragility.

Scott gathered our family to him and said, "We need to pray." There in our circle of six—Scott, me, Zach, Zeke, Rachel, and Gabe—we stood holding each other so tightly we could have all fit in a phone booth. Then Scott cried with our children (what *is* it about a man's tears?) and prayed aloud for the young man's family, whose lives would never again be the same.

Later that night, Scott went for one of his "moonwalks." Out of darkness deep in the woods, he heard a cry—a deep, aching moan—and knew it was someone in pain. He called to the voice, "I'm coming!" There sitting amongst the trees, alone and overcome with grief, was a teenage boy Scott hadn't seen before.

"Son," Scott spoke gently, "would you mind some company?" So Scott sat a long time with the boy-almost-man and listened as he questioned God and the reason we're born, "What, only to die in freak accidents?" After a while, Scott pointed toward the stars and said, "I know it hurts, we're all hurting now. But there *is* more to life than we see. There's Someone up there who loves you and me—and your friend. If your friend had a choice right now, with all he's experiencing beyond those stars, there's no way he'd come back to this sorry old planet of pain."

Now some people might not think of Scott as "spiritual." He doesn't conform to the standard church mold of most men I know who are deacons and elders and such. He's more at home on a mountain than in a church pew; would rather work a piece of wood with his hands, any day, than attend meetings. But he's always been willing without thinking twice, to walk through the woods, toward a soul crying out in the dark. And he loves nothing better, while walking, than talking to the Maker of moonlight and stars. Come to think of it, he reminds me a lot of a certain carpenter's Son.

And this, dear friends, is my husband, my beloved, my friend.

◆ ◆ ◆

Jesus looked at him and loved him.

Mark 10:21

To love another person,
is to see the face of God.

—lyric from Les Misérables

31

The Power of Love

Not long ago, I heard Dr. Beck Wethers, one of the survivors of the ill-fated 1996 Mt. Everest ascent, tell his story. It was a tale I would not soon forget.

Dr. Wethers walked on stage with an easy manner, dressed in khakis, a sports shirt, and a tweed jacket. Part of his nose had been reconstructed, one hand was missing—a metal prosthesis took its place; the other hand was web-like—the lasting results of a frost-bitten nightmare on a relentless, blizzard-whirling mountain of ice.

Dr. Wethers opened his mouth to speak, and involuntarily I dropped my jaw in fascination and didn't close it until he stopped speaking an hour later. Dr. Wethers has not recounted his ordeal so often that it's automatic. His voice still breaks as he recalls friends who died beside him, the despair, and seemingly unending bad turns of events. (He told me, as we visited later, that when he can tell his story without feeling it anymore, he'll cease to speak of it.)

What fascinated me most was what kept Beck Wethers going, what made him get up when everyone else had pronounced him dead. He shared that it was the memory, the vision, of his wife—clear and sweet and poignant—that kept him going. He desperately wanted to hold her and his children in his arms once more.

A second illustration of love's power unfolds from Viktor Frankl's biography and psychological analysis, *Man's Search For Meaning*. In Frankl's soul-stirring account of his time in a concentration camp, he tells of one particularly chilling night. The exhausted prisoners were forced to walk through snow and stones and large puddles, to work frozen ground with pickaxes until morning light. Though few words were spoken, one of the emaciated inmates whispered, "If our wives could see us now! I do hope they are better off in their camps and don't know what is happening to us."

Silence followed the man's remark, but Frankl later wrote, "Each of us was thinking of his wife. Occasionally I looked at the sky where the stars were fading and the pink light of the morning was beginning to spread behind a dark bank of clouds. But my mind clung to my wife's image, imagining it with an uncanny acuteness. I heard her answering me, saw her smile, her frank and encouraging look. Real or not, her look was then more luminous than the sun which was beginning to rise....I understood how a man who has nothing left in this world still may know bliss, be it only for a brief moment, in the contemplation of his beloved... nothing could touch the strength of my love, my thoughts, and the image...."

Tragically, along with six million others, Frankl's young wife died under the Nazi's cruel reign. But Victor beat the odds (only one out of 28 prisoners survived the death camps) and went on to share his insights on the things that give life meaning—even when all human dignities and basic comforts have been stripped away. Next to an abiding faith in God, it was the love of a wife that gave some men strength to rise from their filthy cots to face another pain-filled day, when others gave in to despair, awaiting their dismal fate.

Wethers and Frankl come from different continents, different times, and different circumstances; each was trapped in a desperate place of bitter cold and darkness, with precious little hope.

Interestingly, for both Viktor Frankl and Dr. Beck Wethers, it was the memory of a loving wife that gave these men courage, even brief moments of bliss, in life's most awful moments.

I learned from these two men just how powerful a woman's love for a man can be. Our husbands may not be facing a Nazi prison camp; they might not be fighting for their lives on Everest. But all men, at some time, face hopelessness and exhaustion and a hard-edged world. May we love them enough so the memory of our smiling faces, our "you can make it!" encouragement, keeps them going in the face of adversity.

And husbands, please cherish your wives today. Hold them close. There are thousands of men who would give anything for a chance to enjoy that simple, warm ritual with their beloved once more. Don't take your love for granted. Not this day.

◆ ◆ ◆

Many waters cannot quench love, rivers cannot wash it away.

SONG OF SONGS 8:7

What Matters...

Although I conquer all the earth,

Yet for me there is only one city.

In that city there is for me only one house;

And in that house, one room only;

And in that room, a bed.

And one woman sleeps there,

The shining joy and jewel of all my kingdom.

—Old Sanskrit poem

32

Prayer for Two?

They say raising teenagers is like nailing Jell-O to a tree. Scott and I have discovered the great truth in this cartoon-like visual. We have plans for our kids and are ready to nail them down when suddenly—woops! slurp! slosh!—there goes the kid, with a will of his own, sliding down a path much different from the one we'd envisioned.

This period of parenting keeps us constantly on our toes, and on our knees. More often we are reaching for each other's hands these days, for comfort and assurance of our sanity, and for a quick respite of prayer.

Praying together has not been easy for us. After the honeymoon phase, when we began to uncover each other's faults, it grew more difficult to come to God, as a twosome, in prayer. Felt almost hypocritical. After all, we knew the worst about each other now. How could we join hands and hearts in such a holy act, knowing we were so far from holy ourselves? But desperate times are now calling for desperate

189

measures, and so, to our knees we go. And we are finding that even as our hands clasp in the simple act of acknowledging our helplessness before God, He is binding us together on a deeper level than we've ever known as husband and wife.

A friend recently shared some research about Christian marriages. Oddly enough, just being Christian doesn't seem to reduce the divorce rate. Going to church regularly together did result in slightly more stable marriages. But church-going does not—interestingly enough—appear to bring about a more satisfying relationship, according to this survey. However, couples that prayed together reported enjoying the most satisfying marriages of all and—here's where we need a drumroll—the chance of divorce dropped to less than one percent. THIS is research worth shouting from marriage counseling rooftops!

Recently I spoke at a small church in Tennessee, filled to the steeple with good folks who knew how to pray. Before the ladies' conference, the men had surrounded the church and prayed for the women who would be coming to the retreat. I marveled at the husbands' corporate prayers as they asked God to bring spiritual refreshment to their wives. When I arrived at the church, I was ushered into a small office, surrounded by women who laid hands on me and prayed. Prayer, prayer, everywhere!

It so happened that Scott, who rarely joins me when I travel, came with me to this event. Only God knew how much we needed the prayers of other mothers and fathers at this particular point in our lives. I realize that I am "the speaker," and my ministry is one of bringing laughter and encouragement to others. But there are times when life hurts too much to laugh without some mingling of tears. I come to bless others, but often find myself standing in the need of prayer.

Since I am not the type to suffer in silence, I asked other hurting moms and dads to join Scott and me in praying for our children. As I honestly shared some recent hurts and needs, it was as if the Holy Spirit descended and wrapped His love around us en masse. I've received several notes since that conference inquiring how we are doing, thanking us for being open enough to ask for prayer. One note came today, in fact, saying, "I just wanted thank you for being 'real' with us. It would have been so easy for you to have just covered up your emotional turmoil, but you didn't and that took courage. Sometimes it is so much easier for us to simply wear our masks rather than truly express or show others what we are going through. I'm dealing with this sort of issue right now..."

I wrote her back and thanked her, telling her that when my need is great enough, it overcomes all residual spiritual pride. And since that weekend, we've seen some miraculous answers to our heartfelt prayers.

When we are walking through deep pain, its like being in a fog. It's hard to read Scripture; even harder to pray. And yet we need the Word, and we are desperate for God to move in our life. Like the paralytic who could not walk to Jesus. Sometimes we must rely on our friends, and our mates, to bring our weakened selves to God's throne on the "mattress" of prayer.

For where two or more are gathered in prayer, Jesus promises to always be there. Sometimes I think He even shows up in the loving voices of others praying for us.

Are you hurting today, in any small way? Don't let the sun go down on your pain alone. Reach out to a partner—your husband or wife or a close friend—and tell them, with all vulnerability, that you are standin' in the need of a "two or more" prayer.

Trust me—He'll be there.

◆ ◆ ◆

"Where two or more are gathered together in my name, there I am in their midst."

MATTHEW 18:20

33

Grow Old with Me

I was signing books in Georgia, when a vivacious, older woman, probably in her seventies, began to tell me about her late husband.

"Oh, honey, he was a nut! He'd say, 'Dee, where do you want to go for lunch?'—and he meant what CITY did I want to go to! In our retirement years, he bought an airplane and every day he woke up like a little boy ready for an adventure. He was always teasing me—following me around with a video camera while I exercised, pulling practical jokes—but he also knew how to make me feel like a princess." I couldn't help thinking of a quote I'd read somewhere, perhaps on a card in a gift shop: "Age doesn't protect you from love. But love, to some extent, protects you from age."

Dee wiped a tear from the corner of her eye but managed to keep smiling. "I miss him every day of my life. Sometimes when I see a young couple in church, and the husband lays his hand on his wife's hand—oh, I can hardly take it. Our last years together were so precious. Really, Becky, we were like two kids in love."

Not a month later, I was speaking in Mississippi and chatting with yet another woman in her "golden years." She fairly glowed as she explained, "Our kids and grandkids think we've gone crazy! We moved to the country a few years ago—way off from the city to the middle of the woods. And you know what? We love it! Peace, quiet, stars—each other...." With the words "each other," she patted my arm, winked, and grinned.

After listening to these two women, I re-determined that I'm in my marriage for the long haul, for better or worse, richer or poorer—because I made a vow before God, sure, but also because I don't want to miss the fun ahead. Younger couples need to hear from older married folk, and also from those who've lost their mates. We need reminders that marriage is worth fighting for, working at, toughing out, and clinging to. In the middle of arguments over bills and laundry and kids, we need to envision love-worn hands, intertwined, as we walk into the sunset of life together.

Have you caught a glimpse of *Love in the 90s?* It's a beautiful book—not about love in the decade of the nineties—but about the romance between a man and wife in their tenth decade of life. As I leafed through the adorable candid photos, I gained a much-needed refresher course on The Long-term Perspective of Marriage.

Judith Sills, Ph.D., writes of a conversation with a friend that helped me see, again, the importance of this "long haul perspective" thing.

> "James and I had been married about a year. You know what he's like, so you can imagine how much we had to work out that first year.

"We were taking a little day cruise with my family. I have a clear memory of walking up a bumpy gang-plank, with him walking next to me, snapping at me: 'Watch where you're going.' 'Do you have every-thing?' I clenched inside, not wanting to scream back at him in front of my parents.

"I turned away from him and met the eye of a woman standing right behind us. She was a very old lady. Actually, she looked like one of those wrinkled apple dolls in white tennis sneakers. She smiled and reached over to touch my hand. 'I would give everything I have left,' she said, nodding towards my husband, 'to have mine back, looking out for me just like that.'

"I can't explain why, but...my anger vanished. I felt an overwhelming love for James and a sense of pure, calm happiness. I turned back to him and took his hand and we kept going.[1]"

Are you struggling in your marriage over minor irrita-tions—trying to keep from screaming out in frustration? Maybe this message from the old, wrinkled apple lady will bring new perspective. Perhaps you can quit struggling to change every quirk and annoyance and difference in each other, and instead, accept that some irritating personality traits may never change. So let go of the struggle, lovingly take your mate's hand in yours, and get on with walking (or skipping, or flying) down the Road to the 90s.

◆ ◆ ◆

So they are no longer two, but one. Therefore
what God has joined together, let man not
separate.

MATTHEW 19:6

Grow old along with me!
The best is yet to be,
The last of life,
for which the first was made.

—Robert Browning

Benediction/Dedication

In honor of a marriage
passing through the fire

Jon Walker is my editor at *Home Life* Magazine, where some of these essays first appeared in my monthly "Marriage 9-1-1" column. Jon has always encouraged me through his words but mostly by the kindness, humor, and fairness that radiates from who he is. He and his courageous wife, Sherry, have recently walked through the poignant sadness of carrying to term a baby they knew wouldn't live more than a few hours or days. This has to be one of the most heart-wrenching journeys any couple would have to travel. Jon and Sherry chose to walk it hand in hand with amazing grace their love witnessing to all.

Here is part of an e-mail I received from Jon during their experience:

Dear Friends,

As of this writing, Jeremy is at 33 weeks in my wife's womb. That this little boy with trisomy 18 and spina bifida is still alive has surprised the doctors. This week, as I looked at an ultrasound of our in-utero son, I could see in profile that he is the spitting image of his older brother, Christopher. It's obvious in these pictures that Jeremy is paralyzed from the waist down, yet it's also obvious that God's hand is at the center of all life.

My wife and I are now preparing for the arrival of a son who has been given only a slim chance of survival, but even if we have him for only a few weeks, we will celebrate and gratefully care for the young life entrusted to us by God. Occasionally people comment that they don't think they could handle such a situation. I've taken to jokingly saying, "You're right, you couldn't," but then I go on to explain that it's God's grace poured into us that allows us to embrace Jeremy so joyfully. God has given us His grace for this moment; He doesn't need to give others grace for Jeremy's predicament. And when they go through a trial that I know I couldn't handle, it will be because God poured His grace into their lives and not mine.

Jon and Sherry cherished baby Jeremy every day he lived in the safety of his mother's womb. He died at birth on August 5, 1999. Yet his small, brief life pulled compassion and prayers from hundreds of men, women, and children who prayed for the Walker family.

It is with great honor that I dedicate this book to Jeremy Clark Walker, and to his parents who loved him before he ever drew breath—and who love him still as he plays with the angels under God's watchful smile.

Now, to the Walker Family, from our family, this is our prayer of hope and blessing for you in the days and years to come:

◆ ◆ ◆

May the Lord bless and protect you, may the Lord's face radiate with joy because of you; may he be gracious to you, show you his favor, and give you his peace

NUMBERS 6:24 TLB

◆ ◆ ◆

A Memorial in Jeremy's name is set up at:

Cumberland Crisis Pregnancy Center
625 Johnny Cash Parkway
Hendersonville, TN 37075

Notes

All quotations, unless otherwise noted, are from *Words of Love II,* edited by Tina Reed (Berkley, 1994); *Quotations on Love,* compiled by Rosalie Maggior (Prentice Hall, 1997); or the Internet.

Chapter 1
1. Anne Lamott, *Traveling Mercies* (New York, New York: Pantheon Books, 1999).

Chapter 3
1. Michelle Weiner-Davis, *A Woman's Guide to Changing Her Man* (New York, New York: Golden Books, 1998).

Chapter 13
1. Dr. Willard F. Harley, Jr., *His Needs, Her Needs: Building an Affair-proof Marriage* (Grand Rapids, Michigan: Revell, 1994). p. 14.

Chapter 18
1. Harley, Ibid.

Chapter 19
1. Ken Gire, *The Reflective Life* (Colorado Springs, Colorado: Chariot Victor, 1998).

Chapter 29
1. Erma Bombeck, *Forever, Erma* (Kansas City, Kansas: Andrews and McMell Publishing; 1997).

Chapter 33
1. Judith Sills, *Loving Men More, Needing Men Less* (New York, New York: Penguin Books, 1996).

◆ ◆ ◆

For information about Becky's other books and speaking schedule, check out her website at www.beckyfreeman.com.

E-mail Gene Kent at speakupinc@aol.com for information about having Becky speak at your retreat, conference or special event.

◆ ◆ ◆

Other Books Authored or Coauthored By Becky Freeman

Worms in My Tea and Other Mixed Blessings

Adult Children of Fairly Functional Parents

Marriage 911

Still Lickin' the Spoon

A View from the Porch Swing

Real Magnolias

Courage for the Chicken Hearted

Egg-stra Courage for the Chicken Hearted

Available from your local Christian bookstore